HBJ BOOKMARK READING PROGRAM, EAGLE EDITION

Margaret Early
Elizabeth K. Cooper
Nancy Santeusanio

Level 9

Ring Around the World

WIDENING CIRCLES
- RING AROUND THE WORLD

HARCOURT BRACE JOVANOVICH, PUBLISHERS

New York   Chicago   San Francisco   Atlanta   Dallas   and   *London*

Cover: J. Nicholson/Focus on Sports

Copyright © 1983, 1979 by Harcourt Brace Jovanovich, Inc.
All rights reserved. No part of this publication may be reproduced or transmitted in any form or by any means, electronic or mechanical, including photocopy, recording, or any information storage and retrieval system, without permission in writing from the publisher.

Requests for permission to make copies of any part of the work should be mailed to:
Permissions, Harcourt Brace Jovanovich, Inc., 757 Third Avenue, New York, NY 10017

Printed in the United States of America   ISBN 0-15-331259-9

ACKNOWLEDGMENTS: For permission to reprint copyrighted material, grateful acknowledgment is made to the following sources:

The Bobbs-Merrill Company, Inc.: Adapted from "Miguel and the Baker" (retitled: "Anna and the Baker") from *Folk Tales of Latin America* by Shirlee P. Newman. Copyright © 1962 by Bobbs-Merrill Company, Inc.
Curtis Brown, Ltd.: "The Cattle Egret" from *When the Stones Were Soft* by Eleanor B. Heady. Text copyright © 1968 by Eleanor B. Heady.
William Collins & World Publishing Co., Inc.: *Taro and the Tofu* by Masako Matsuno. Copyright © 1962 by Masako Matsuno.
Coward, McCann & Geoghegan, Inc.: Adapted from *Nate the Great and the Lost List* (retitled: "Nate the Great") by Marjorie Weinman Sharmat. Text copyright © 1975 by Marjorie Weinman Sharmat. Adaptation by Susan Smith based upon the book *Amelia Earhart: First Lady of Flight* by Peggy Mann. Copyright © 1970 by Peggy Mann.
Elsevier/Nelson Books: Adapted from "The Case of the Rubber Pillow" from *Encyclopedia Brown Finds the Clues* by Donald J. Sobol. Copyright 1966 by Donald J. Sobol.
Harcourt Brace Jovanovich, Inc.: Adapted from "The Counting of the Crocodiles" from *The Tiger's Whisker and Other Tales and Legends from Asia and the Pacific,* by Harold Courlander. © 1959 by Harold Courlander.
Hart Publishing Company, Inc.: "Unbelievable Animals" from *Incredible Animals* by James Meyers. Copyright 1976 by Hart Publishing Company, Inc.
Holt, Rinehart and Winston, Publishers: Adapted from "The Piper Came to Our Town" from *A Scottish Songbook* by Sorche NicLeodhas. Copyright © 1969 by Leclaire G. Alger.
Houghton Mifflin Company: "A Song of Greatness" from *The Children Sing in the Far West* by Mary Austin. Copyright renewed 1956 by Kenneth M. Chapman and Mary C. Wheelwright.
Johnson Reprint Corporation: "Dream Song" from *The American Indians and Their Music* by Frances Densmore.
William I. Kaufman: "Dragonfly," anonymous, and "Bon Voyage," anonymous Mexican, from *UNICEF Book of Children's Poems* by William I. Kaufman.
J. B. Lippincott Company: "Ring Around the World" from *All Through the Year* by Annette Wynne. Copyright 1932, © renewed 1960 by Annette Wynne.
Harold Ober Associates Incorporated: Adapted from "A Brave Explorer" from *The First Book of Negroes* by Langston Hughes. Copyright © 1960 by Franklin Watts, Inc.
Pantheon Books, a Division of Random House, Inc., and Collins Publishers: Adapted from *Elsa,* by Joy Adamson. Copyright © 1961 by Joy Adamson.
Plays, Inc.: "Little Mouse-Deer" from *Plays from Folktales of Africa and Asia,* by Barbara Winther. Copyright © 1975 by Plays, Inc. This play is for reading purposes only. For permission to perform or produce this play, write to Plays, Inc., 8 Arlington St., Boston, MA 02116.
Prentice-Hall, Inc.: "Mystery of Oak Island" from *Unnatural Resources: True Stories of American Treasure* by Dale M. Titler. © 1973 by Dale M. Titler.
Scholastic Magazines, Inc.: Adapted from "The Story of Christopher Columbus" from *Christopher Columbus* by Ann McGovern. Copyright © 1962 by Ann McGovern.
Charles Scribner's Sons: From *Robbie and the Sled Dog Race* (retitled: "Robin and the Sled Dog Race") by Sara Machetanz. Copyright © 1964 by Sara Machetanz.
Viking Penguin, Inc.: Adapted from *Wee Gillis* by Munro Leaf. Copyright 1938 by Munro Leaf and Robert Lawson, © renewed 1966 by Munro Leaf and John W. Boyd.

Steven Assel: 142–143; Richard Brown: 10–16; Victoria Chess: 9; Kinuko Craft: 36–43; Renée Daily: 8; Diane Dawson: 22–35; Pamela Ford: 106; Shelly Freshman: 98–105; Michael Garland: 161; George Gershinowitz: 80–86; Judy Glasser: 205–211; Conrad Hack: 184–189; Meryl Henderson: 171; Tad Krumeich: 225, 238–242, 244–245, 249; Mila Lazarevich: 97; Dora Leder: 130–141; Jared Lee: 62–64, 93–96, 159, 160, 190–192; Mike Marian: 162–170; Frank Mayo: 72–79, 193, 227, 228, 256; Yoshi Miyaki: 182–183; Carol Nicklaus: 17–21; Oni: 87–92, 226, 233–237; Alan Reingold: 261–275; Frank Riley: 115–129; Lino Saffioti: 250, 251, 254, 255; Ruth Sanderson: 172–181; Miriam Schottland: 44–49; Chris Spollen: 66–71; Krystina Stasiak: 50–61; Roz Streifer: 107; Kyuzo Tsugami: 65, 144–158; Lane Yerkes: 194–201.

HBJ PHOTOS: pages 202, 203

Page 108, The Metropolitan Museum of Art; 109, Reproduced with permission of the West Baffin Eskimo Co-operative, Copyright, 1968; 110, Instituto Nacional de Bellas Artes, Mexico; 111, The Brooklyn Museum, Gift of Mr. and Mrs. Robert E. Blum, Mr. and Mrs. Alastair B. Martin, Mr. and Mrs. Donald M. Oenslager, Mrs. Florence E. Blum Fund; 112, The Tate Gallery, London; 113, Scala/EPA Inc.; 114, Sekai Bunka Photo; 229, Arthur Tress/Photo Researchers; 230, from "World without Sun," © Jacques-Yves Cousteau; 231, Scripps Institution of Oceanography; 232, Rich Chesher/Photo Researchers; 243, 247, Ben Kocivar Photos; 246, 248, Courtesy of Grumman Aerospace Corp.; 252, 253, NASA; 256, Photo Ben Mayer.

Contents

Ring Around the World (POEM) ——— 8
   by Annette Wynne

Tales from Everywhere ——— 9

How Things Came to Be ——— 10
   How the Camel Got Its Hump ——— 10
     (FABLE)
     by Rudyard Kipling
   The Counting of the Crocodiles ——— 17
     (FABLE)
     by Harold Courlander

Anna and the Baker (STORY) ——— 22
   by Shirlee P. Newman
   The Case Against Anna ——— 28

Yuji and the Ocean (STORY) ——— 36
   by Jim Tobin

The Cattle Egret   (STORY) —————————— 44
   by Eleanor B. Heady
Little Mouse-Deer   (PLAY) —————————— 50
   by Barbara Winther
     Act 1: Mouse-Deer and Tiger ————— 51
     Act 2: Mouse-Deer and the Deep Pit — 57
Skills Lesson: Syllables ———————————— 62

Strange As It Seems ———————————— 65

The King Who Was *Never* Wrong   (STORY) — 66
Mystery of Oak Island   (INFORMATION) ——— 72
   by Dale Titler
   Discovery ——————————————————— 72
   More People Try ———————————————— 77
   Oak Island Today ——————————————— 79
Unbelievable Animals   (INFORMATION) ——— 80
   by James Meyers
   Longest-Lived Animals of All ——————— 80
   High Jumpers and Far Travelers ————— 81
   Other Unbelievable Animals ——————— 84
Harry Houdini, Master Magician ————— 87
   (BIOGRAPHY)
   The Man No Locks Could Hold ————— 88
   Escape from the Packing Crate ————— 90
Skills Lesson: Topic and Main Idea ————— 93

Look All Around You — 97

Camel Girl (STORY) — 98
by Elizabeth Cooper

Poems by Children — 106
- Dragonfly — 106
- Bon Voyage — 107

Art Around the World (INFORMATION) — 108

Robin and the Sled Dog Race (STORY) — 115
by Sara Machetanz

Wee Gillis (STORY) — 130
by Munro Leaf

The Piper Came to Our Town — 142
(TRADITIONAL SCOTTISH SONG)

Taro and the Tofu (STORY) — 144
by Masako Matsuno

Skills Lesson: Reading Maps — 159

Explorers — 161

The Story of Christopher Columbus — 162
(BIOGRAPHY)
by Ann McGovern
- Sailing the Sea of Darkness — 162
- "Turn Back! Turn Back!" — 164
- "Land Ahoy! Land Ahoy!" — 168

Dream Song —————————————— 171
    (SIOUXIAN MEDICINE SONG)
Amelia Earhart, First Lady of Flight —— 172
    (BIOGRAPHY)
    Adapted by Susan Smith
A Song of Greatness (POEM) ————— 182
    by Mary Austin
A Brave Explorer (BIOGRAPHY) ———— 184
    by Langston Hughes
Skills Lesson: Topical Organization —— 190

World of Mystery —————————— 193

The Case of the Rubber Pillow (STORY) — 194
    by Donald J. Sobol
Sound Effects for a Radio Play ———— 202
    (INFORMATION)
    by Dina Anastasio
The Haunted House: A Radio Play —— 205
    by Dina Anastasio
Nate the Great (STORY) ——————— 212
    by Marjorie Weinman Sharmat
Skills Lesson: Fact and Opinion ——— 222

Today and Tomorrow ——————— 225

Tomorrow's World ————————— 226

Tomorrow: Exploring the Sea — 227
   (INFORMATION)
     Underwater Craft — 229
     Living Under the Sea — 233

Tomorrow: Moving Around — 238
   (INFORMATION)
     New Kinds of Trains — 243
     New Planes — 245
     Watercraft — 247

Tomorrow: Voyages to the Islands of Light — 250
   (INFORMATION)
   by Richard M. Crum
     Yesterday — 250
     Today — 253
     Tomorrow — 254

Skills Lesson: Sequence, Time Order — 257

Bonus Book

Elsa — 261
   by Joy Adamson

Glossary — 276

New Words — 285

(To be read by the teacher.)

Ring Around the World

Ring around the world
Taking hands together
All across the temperate
And the torrid weather.
Past the royal palm-trees
By the ocean sand
Make a ring around the world
Taking each other's hand;
In the valleys, on the hill,
Over the prairie spaces,
There's a ring around the world
Made of children's friendly faces.

ANNETTE WYNNE

Tales from Everywhere

How Things Came to Be

How the Camel Got Its Hump

by RUDYARD KIPLING

Now this tale tells us how the Camel got its hump.

In the beginning of years, when the world was so new-and-all, the animals were just beginning to work for people. Among the animals was a Camel, and it lived in the desert. It did not want to work. So it chewed on sticks and shrubs, and when anybody spoke to it, the Camel said "Humph!" and no more.

The Horse came to the Camel on the first morning. It had a bit in its mouth. The Horse

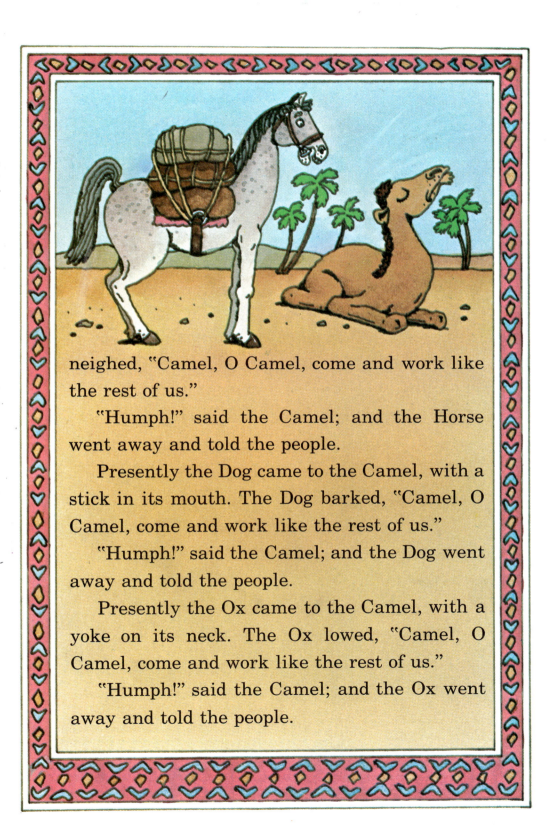

neighed, "Camel, O Camel, come and work like the rest of us."

"Humph!" said the Camel; and the Horse went away and told the people.

Presently the Dog came to the Camel, with a stick in its mouth. The Dog barked, "Camel, O Camel, come and work like the rest of us."

"Humph!" said the Camel; and the Dog went away and told the people.

Presently the Ox came to the Camel, with a yoke on its neck. The Ox lowed, "Camel, O Camel, come and work like the rest of us."

"Humph!" said the Camel; and the Ox went away and told the people.

At the end of the day, a Man called the Horse and the Dog and the Ox together. He said, "Three, O Three, I'm very sorry for you (with the world so new-and-all). That Humph-thing in the desert can't work, or it would have been here by now. So I am going to leave it there; you must work harder to make up for it."

That made the Three very angry (with the world so new-and-all). They talked among themselves on the rim of the desert. The Camel came, chewing on a twig, and laughed at them. Then it said "Humph!" and went away again.

Presently there came along the Djinn of All Deserts, rolling upon a grey cloud. (Djinns always ride that way because it is Magic.) He stopped to talk with the Three.

"Djinn of All Deserts," said the Horse, "is it right for anyone to be idle, with the world so new-and-all?"

"Of course not," said the Djinn.

"Well," said the Horse, "there's a thing in your desert. It has a long neck and long legs, and it hasn't done a bit of work since the very first morning."

"Well," said the Djinn, whistling, "that's my Camel, for all the gold in the desert! What does it say about it?"

"It says 'Humph!'" said the Dog. "And it won't do a bit of work."

"Does it say anything else?"

"Only 'Humph!'" said the Ox.

"Very good," said the Djinn. "Will you three kindly wait here?"

The Djinn rolled himself up in the grey cloud and flew across the desert and found the Camel looking at itself in a pool of water.

The Djinn sat down, with his chin in his hand. He began to think a Great Magic. The Camel looked at itself in the pool of water.

"From the first morning you've given the Three your own work to do," said the Djinn. He went on thinking Magics, with his chin resting in his hand.

"Humph!" said the Camel.

"I shouldn't say that again if I were you," said the Djinn. "You might say it one time too many. Obey me now. I want you to work."

And the Camel said "Humph!" again. But no sooner had it said that than the Camel saw its back, which it was so proud of, puffing up and puffing up into a great big humph.

"Do you see that?" said the Djinn. "That's your very own humph that you've brought upon yourself by not working. You've done no work since the first day when the work began. Now you are going to work."

"How can I," said the Camel, "with this humph on my back?"

"That's there," said the Djinn, "because you missed those three days. Now you will be able

to work for three days without eating, because you can live on your humph. And don't you ever say I never did anything for you. Obey me now. Come out of the desert and go to the Three and behave yourself!"

And the Camel, humph and all, went away to join the Three. And from that day to this, the Camel always wears a humph. (We call it a "hump" now, not to hurt its feelings.) But it has never yet caught up with the three days that it missed at the beginning of the world. And it has never yet learned how to behave.

The Counting of the Crocodiles

by HAROLD COURLANDER

On the island of Oki in ancient times, there lived a hare who longed to go to the mainland. He wished to live a better life, for the island of Oki was small and life there was very boring. The hare often sat on the beach, looking longingly across the water at the mainland.

One day while he sat there, a crocodile lifted its head out of the water and looked hungrily at the hare.

"Why do you stare at the king of hares?" the hare said. "Have you no manners?"

"King of hares?" the crocodile said. "That is laughable."

"Do not show your foolishness," the hare answered. "I rule more hares than there are crocodiles from here to the mainland."

"That is silly," the crocodile said. "Do you have any idea how many of us there are hidden below the water?"

"Yes, there are only a few compared to the number of hares that obey me."

The crocodile shouted in anger. "Oh, foolish hare! If you were to see all the crocodiles who swim in the sea, you would scream in fear!"

"Very well, let me see them," the hare said.

So the crocodile went below the water. In a short time many crocodiles came up to the top of the water. More and more rose, until the water was covered with them.

The first crocodile rose again and said to the hare, "Now you may choke on your words. Have you ever seen so many crocodiles?"

"No," the hare said, "I have never seen so many crocodiles. But still they are not as many as the hares."

"You lie," the crocodile said. "There are more crocodiles!"

"Very well, we shall count the crocodiles, then the hares. Tell your friends to move more closely together so that we may begin."

And when the crocodiles had moved more closely together, the hare jumped on the back of one and called out "One." He jumped on the back of the next and called out "Two." Each number that he called, the crocodiles repeated after him. The hare jumped from back to back toward the mainland. "One hundred twenty," he called. "One hundred twenty," the crocodiles answered.

When he was near the shore of the mainland, the hare stood on the back of the last crocodile and shouted, "Oh, silly crocodiles! How vain you are! All you have done is to make a bridge for me to the mainland!" Then he leaped for the land. But the last crocodile, hearing the unkind words, quickly snapped his jaws and bit off the hare's tail.

Though the hare was safe, he had lost his tail by talking too soon.

So it is that the hare has only a stump of a tail today, where once it was long and bushy.

Anna and the Baker

by SHIRLEE P. NEWMAN

Anna owned a store and lived in a little house in the city. From morning till night she worked in her store. Though she worked hard and grew weary, her neighbors could always say, "No one has a happier smile than Anna."

Only the baker, who lived in the next building, was too busy to tell whether Anna smiled or not. Now the baker was a very hardworking man, and he made wonderful cakes. He had plenty of money. And every night he counted the money. He loved money so much, it took him hours to count it, as he touched each coin lovingly and put it in a pile.

Though the baker hardly ever spoke to her, Anna felt herself lucky to live next door to the bake shop. When she got up in the morning, Anna would open her window wide. She would enjoy the beautiful smell of newly baked bread and cakes.

One morning while Anna was sniffing the smells, the baker walked outside his shop for a bit of air. Looking up, he saw Anna at her window. The baker's face grew red and angry. "What right does Anna have to enjoy the smells of my baking for free?" he thought. "Anna!" he called out. "It's time you paid me for smelling my bread and cakes each morning."

Anna laughed and said, "You are having fun, Baker! Ha ha, I didn't know you could be so funny!" And Anna leaned out the window and sniffed some more.

"Fun?" the baker roared. "This is not fun! I work the whole night in my shop. I use the finest flour, the best milk to make wonderful things. Why should you enjoy their smells and pay me nothing for it?"

"Why, he is serious," Anna thought. "How funny! He seriously thinks I should pay him for the smells that come from his shop!"

Anna could not help herself — she started to laugh. She laughed and laughed and laughed! She roared and rolled on the floor! She held her sides and laughed some more!

One by one the other neighbors leaned out the windows. "What's going on?" the woman up the street said. "What's so funny?"

Anna could hardly talk for laughing so hard. "The baker — he — he thinks I should pay him for smelling his breads and cakes!"

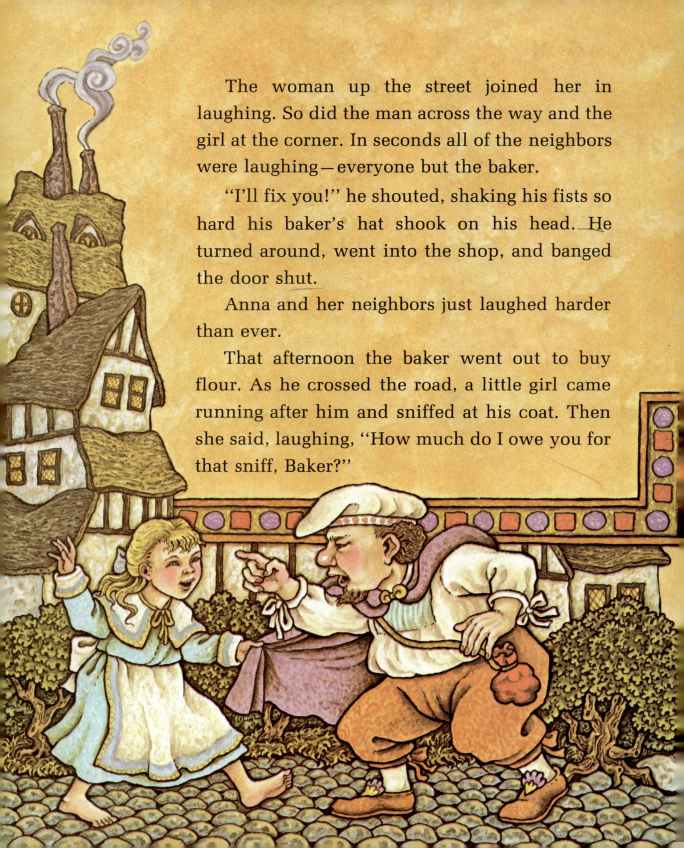

The woman up the street joined her in laughing. So did the man across the way and the girl at the corner. In seconds all of the neighbors were laughing—everyone but the baker.

"I'll fix you!" he shouted, shaking his fists so hard his baker's hat shook on his head. He turned around, went into the shop, and banged the door shut.

Anna and her neighbors just laughed harder than ever.

That afternoon the baker went out to buy flour. As he crossed the road, a little girl came running after him and sniffed at his coat. Then she said, laughing, "How much do I owe you for that sniff, Baker?"

Soon some boys joined in the fun. Following the baker around the corner, they laughed and shouted. Now the baker was angrier than ever! "Everyone is making fun of me! There's just one thing to do—I'll go to court and see the judge."

The judge listened to the baker's story quietly. Not once did she laugh, or even smile.

"So, Judge," the baker finished, "Anna is guilty. She has enjoyed the smells of my baking for years, and never has she paid me so much as one silver coin."

"Hmm," the judge said, "I see what you mean. I shall go over the case carefully and decide fairly."

The baker thanked the judge and went home.

The Case Against Anna

Three days later a court paper was put up in the town.

"THE CASE OF BAKER AGAINST ANNA," the paper read.

"THE TWO MUST COME BEFORE THE JUDGE TOMORROW. ANNA MUST BRING TO COURT A HUNDRED SILVER COINS."

"What shall I do?" Anna thought when she saw the court paper. "I don't even have five silver coins."

28

But that night the woman from down the street knocked on Anna's door and handed Anna a bag of coins.

"Thank you, dear friend," said Anna, "but if I am found guilty and must pay, how will I ever pay you back?"

The woman said, "The coins are yours, for all your friends joined together to give them to you. Don't worry about paying them back."

Anna said, "I will pay you back if it takes all my life!"

The next morning the courtroom was filled with people. The judge came in and quieted everyone down. "Baker," she said, "rise and tell your side of the case."

The baker got to his feet. Not taking his eyes off the bag of money in Anna's hands, he spoke. "All my life I have worked hard, Judge," he said. "I bake the finest of breads, the lightest of cakes. Every morning Anna opens her window and sniffs the wonderful smells from my ovens.

"Is this fair?" the baker went on. "I ask you, Judge, is it fair that I work so hard while my neighbor Anna sits at her window and enjoys the wonderful smells—free?"

The judge looked serious.

The baker shook his head. "No," he said, "it is not fair, and so I should be paid."

The judge listened to every word. Then she said, "How much do you think you should be paid, Baker?"

The baker smiled and said, "Well, Judge, I think a hundred silver coins would be about right." The baker sat down.

The judge turned to Anna and said slowly, "Rise, Anna."

Her legs shaking, Anna rose.

"Well, Anna, are you guilty?" asked the judge. "Do the smells of newly baked bread and cakes come to your window every day?"

"Yes, Judge, they do."

"And are the smells good smells or bad smells?" asked the judge.

"Good smells," Anna said.

The judge rapped on the table and said, "You are guilty of enjoying the smells from the baker's shop, so you must hand the bag of coins to him."

The room was quiet as Anna did so. The baker took the money bag; turning to leave, he said, "Thank you, Judge!"

"Oh, just one second, Baker. Let's see whether all the money is there," said the judge. "Take the money from the bag and count it."

The baker untied the bag and the coins fell to the table. The baker smiled—how those silver coins glowed in the sunlight! How prettily they rang as they bounced about!

Slowly, one by one, the baker counted the shiny silver coins. Then he returned the coins to the bag.

"There are a hundred, Judge," he said. "Thank you." He started to leave.

"Oh, just one second, Baker," said the judge. "Give the bag of money back to Anna."

Anna stared in surprise. So did the baker. So did everyone else.

The judge rose and said, "In the name of the people of our city, I shall now decide the case of Baker against Anna."

Everyone sat very still, listening.

"You, Anna," said the judge, "have enjoyed the smell of the baker's goods; you, Baker, have enjoyed the feel of Anna's money. The case is now closed."

The courtroom was still. A few seconds passed, and then suddenly someone in the back of the room started to laugh. Someone else joined in. Now the whole courtroom was flooded with laughter!

"Hurray for Anna!"

As she listened, Anna suddenly understood the meaning of the judge's words. She had won—she owed the baker nothing!

Smiling, Anna handed the bag of money to her friends.

"Now I owe no one!" she cried.

"Yes!" her friends shouted, "and you can sniff the baker's goods as much as you want!" Laughing and cheering, the people marched out of the courtroom.

The room was quiet now. The judge sat back in her chair, looking serious. Then all at once her face broke into a smile. She started to laugh. She laughed and laughed and laughed; she roared and rolled on the floor; she held her sides and laughed some more!

"Tomorrow morning I shall go see Anna," she thought. "I'd like to enjoy those wonderful smells, too!"

Yuji and the Ocean

by JIM TOBIN

Yuji pushed the dark soil against the sides of the young bamboo plant. "That will hold you in place, little one," the boy said, smiling.

The smile disappeared as Yuji looked back at his mother and the rest of the people in the village.

"We are all like plants," the boy cried. "We live here in the heart of Japan and never leave the forest. We stay in this forest as if we were planted here."

Suddenly a voice behind Yuji roared with laughter. "And where would you go if you were not like a plant?"

Yuji turned around to see a giant plant shaking with laughter. "But . . . but you are a bamboo plant!" the boy shouted.

The bamboo answered, "Yes, and I am magic. I am getting tired of this place. Where shall we go?"

"I have heard tales of a distant and

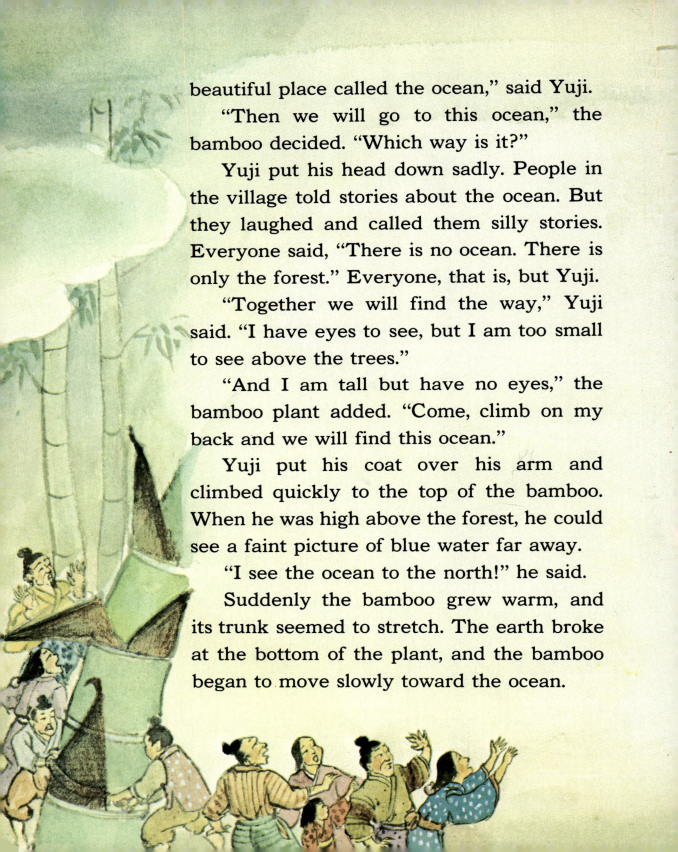

beautiful place called the ocean," said Yuji.

"Then we will go to this ocean," the bamboo decided. "Which way is it?"

Yuji put his head down sadly. People in the village told stories about the ocean. But they laughed and called them silly stories. Everyone said, "There is no ocean. There is only the forest." Everyone, that is, but Yuji.

"Together we will find the way," Yuji said. "I have eyes to see, but I am too small to see above the trees."

"And I am tall but have no eyes," the bamboo plant added. "Come, climb on my back and we will find this ocean."

Yuji put his coat over his arm and climbed quickly to the top of the bamboo. When he was high above the forest, he could see a faint picture of blue water far away.

"I see the ocean to the north!" he said.

Suddenly the bamboo grew warm, and its trunk seemed to stretch. The earth broke at the bottom of the plant, and the bamboo began to move slowly toward the ocean.

When the people in the village spied the walking plant, they screamed. Yuji's mother cried, "Someone stop the monster!"

Everyone rushed after the bamboo plant. Suddenly, just outside the forest, it came to a stop. "We must get Yuji down!" the people of the village cried. But just then the bamboo plant began to fall, for it was too tired to go on. Yuji's mother shrieked as the bamboo leaned to the right and then fell through the air.

"Whoosh" came the sound of the bamboo, falling, falling. "Swoosh" came the sound of the bamboo as it plowed through the tops of small pine trees. And then came

the terrible "Thump!" as the bamboo plant landed.

Yuji's mother and the rest of the people from the village raced toward Yuji. Everyone thought he was hurt because he was not moving. Tears visited everyone's faces, and all the people began to cry.

Then Yuji's eyes opened, and he began to speak. "Did we find it?"

"Find what?" Yuji's mother asked.

"The ocean," Yuji answered. "We were looking for the ocean."

The people of the village laughed for a second. They thought, "The ocean is just a story. Yuji must have hit his head. There is no ocean. There is only forest."

The laughter died down as soon as the people began to look around them. They had followed the trunk of the giant bamboo to find Yuji, but they had found the ocean as well. The sand and sea stretched as far as the eye could measure.

"It is the ocean!" cried Yuji.

The people who were once so afraid to move away from their forest were now running up and down the beach. Some of them even jumped into the water with all their clothes on. One young girl found something wonderful.

"Oh!" she cried and pulled out something small from her pocket. "What is it?" she asked.

"It's a fish," answered Yuji's mother happily. "I remember my grandmother telling me about fish. She said that you could cook and eat them."

"Then I shall catch enough for all of us,"

the girl said as she ran back into the ocean.

The only one who was not happy was Yuji. He had lost a friend. The old bamboo plant had carried him to the ocean, but would never stand on its shore.

"I will never try to find anything new again," Yuji cried.

"Yes, you will," his mother said.

"And you will use your friend again."

She bent down and pulled some bamboo from the giant plant. "Here," she said. "Use the bamboo to build a boat."

Since that time, Yuji's people lived both in the forest and at the shore. They were no longer afraid of change. As for Yuji, the storytellers say that he found the end of the ocean in his bamboo boat. No one knows for sure.

The Cattle Egret
by ELEANOR B. HEADY

Nupe the cattle egret lives in the pastures with herds of cattle. He follows them where they go, sometimes sitting on their backs for a better look at the world.

But Nupe did not *always* live with the cattle. This is how it began.

Once, many years ago, no rain fell for a long time. The rivers stopped running, and the wells were dry. Plants blackened and died in the glare of the sun. Then the stores of food were gone, so people and animals could find nothing to eat or drink.

Kanda the chief saw the despair around him. He called all the people, animals, birds, and insects together in the village.

"We must find water," said the chief. "If any of you can find water, you will earn a great reward from me. I will make you chief of your kind, be you person, animal, bird, or insect." When the chief had finished talking, there was not a sound in the village.

Then softly from his perch on a bush, Nupe the egret spoke. "I will try to get water. I can lose nothing by trying."

A cheer went up from the dry throats of all who were in the village. "Nupe, Nupe, good luck to you, Nupe."

"Please begin at once," urged Kanda the chief, "for we can't wait much longer."

"Do not despair," said Nupe. Nupe flew to the dry bed of a river, where he began to dig with his beak, saying, "I will peck, peck, peck until water comes."

He pecked around and around, making a deep hole. All the people, animals, birds, and insects came to watch and cheer him on. Finally the egret brought up mud on his beak. The watchers stood closer, talking and pointing.

"Please don't crowd," said Nupe as he stopped to rest. "I'll need a lot of room and air if I am to dig down to the water. I'll peck, peck, peck until I have found water for everyone, but you must wait. My beak is small and water is far down in the earth."

Everyone moved away to give the egret room to work. All day he pecked until he had made a very deep hole and was so far down that no one could see him.

Kanda the chief looked over the side of the hole and asked, "Have you found the water yet, Nupe?"

"There should be much water soon, for it is wet here now," said Nupe.

That very second a clear stream of water gushed up, rising into the air and splashing Nupe. He flew up from the hole while Kanda shouted, "Nupe has found water!"

The people and animals almost fell over each other in their rush to the hole.

"Wait! Wait!" urged the chief. "Nupe found the water, so let him drink first."

The weary egret drank his fill, letting the water run down his dry throat. Then one by one, for all the hours until sundown, came the people, the animals, the birds, and the tiny insects to drink from the well.

The air was loud with cheers for the egret. "Nupe has saved us, and so Nupe will be chief of all the birds!"

While all this was happening, Nupe sat in a tree, watching and thinking. "Chief of the birds? No, I'd want to have a free life."

When all had finished drinking, Chief Kanda called them together again.

"Now we must give Nupe his reward. Come, friend, so that I may make you chief of all the birds."

"But I do not wish to be chief," said the egret. "Give me some other reward, something less likely to make trouble."

"Not be chief?" said Kanda. "I cannot understand that."

"I like a free and quiet life," said Nupe. "A chief cannot have that."

"Well, then, what would you like?"

"Only some cattle for my own," said Nupe.

"All you want is a herd of cattle?"

"Yes, Chief Kanda," said Nupe, "for cattle are such lovely, quiet beasts."

"He can have all my cattle if he wishes," shouted a person in the crowd. Others called out, "Yes, yes, all our cattle."

"You may take any cattle in the land because you have found the water," said the chief. "You may live with them in peace; you and your children will guard the cattle."

"Thank you, kind chief," said Nupe, and he flew away and perched happily on the back of a spotted cow.

To this day the egrets live in the pastures with the cattle, playing and feeding beside them or sitting on their backs in the sunshine.

Reprinted from *Plays from Folktales of Africa and Asia*, by Barbara Winther. Copyright © 1975 by Plays, Inc. This play is for reading purposes only. For permission to perform or produce this play, write to Plays, Inc., 8 Arlington St., Boston, MA 02116.

LITTLE MOUSE-DEER

by BARBARA WINTHER

Storyteller 1	(xylophone)	A man
Storyteller 2	(bells)	Mouse-deer
Storyteller 3	(drum)	Tiger
Storyteller 4	(sticks)	Monkey
Storyteller 5	(gong/drum)	Elephant
Storyteller 6	(gong set)	Boar

Setting: the rainforest. Storytellers 1, 2, and 3 come in with xylophone, bells, and drum and sit on floor at one side. Storytellers' music goes with the actions of the players, but they do not play while the actors speak. Actors pantomime actions in a slow, dancelike way.

ACT 1
MOUSE-DEER AND TIGER

STORYTELLER 1: In the rainforest lives a tiny animal that has the face of a mouse and the legs of a deer.
(Storyteller 2 plays bells.)

STORYTELLER 2: Sly little Mouse-deer runs through the forest and stops to drink at a deep pool of water.
(Mouse-deer, carrying bag, comes in, darts about, and sniffs. Bells play. She leans down and pantomimes drinking from pool.)

STORYTELLER 3: Not far behind comes Tiger.
(Tiger charges in, growling softly as Storyteller 3 plays drums.)

51

STORYTELLER 2: Mouse-deer finds some fruit trees and starts to eat.

(Mouse-deer jumps and pantomimes getting fruit and eating it.)

MOUSE-DEER: M-m-m, good, I'll pick some more of this fruit to take home with me.

(Pantomimes picking fruit and filling bag.)

TIGER: How dare you take my fruit! Oooo, I'm getting angrier and angrier!

(Tiger puffs himself up and lifts front claws. Drums and bells play fast.)

MOUSE-DEER (whirls): Tiger! Nice day, is it not?

TIGER (sneers): Not nice at all! I'm hungry.

MOUSE-DEER: Dear me, I'm sorry to hear that.

TIGER: Yes, I'm hungry for the one who eats fruit from my trees.

MOUSE-DEER (looks about): Oh, dear, dear, you must mean me.

(Tiger nods and looks at claws as he pushes them in and out.)

STORYTELLER 2: Mouse-deer tries hard to think of a trick.

(Mouse-deer jumps in the air, smiling.)

MOUSE-DEER: I know what to do! (*to* Tiger) Tiger, you mustn't touch me.

TIGER: Why not?

MOUSE-DEER: Because I can turn one into two.

TIGER: That's silly—nobody can do that.

MOUSE-DEER: Say what you like, but I've been working all morning making two of one. That's why I was picking your fruit—to double it.

TIGER: Double my fruit?

MOUSE-DEER: Of course. Why, this morning I turned one monkey into two; and this afternoon the King wants me to make two of him.

TIGER (*to himself*): Hmm—if there were two of me, I could hunt faster and sleep longer. Mouse-deer, make two of me.

MOUSE-DEER (*shakes head*): No, no, you couldn't stand the force of my magic.

TIGER: Yes, I could. Please!

MOUSE-DEER: Sorry, I have no time . . . I mustn't keep the King waiting.

TIGER: Please, Mouse-deer, please *make* time!

MOUSE-DEER: Well . . . all right. But, you must do everything I tell you.

TIGER: Yes, yes.

MOUSE-DEER: First, close your eyes, then put this bag over your head.

(*Mouse-deer pantomimes taking fruit from bag, then gives bag to Tiger, who puts it on his head.*)

MOUSE-DEER: Next, count slowly backwards from ten to one.

(*Mouse-deer laughs softly, then tiptoes away.*)

TIGER: Ten, nine, eight, seven, six, five, four, three, two, one . . . . Mouse-deer, what do I do now? . . . Mouse-deer, where are you? . . . Mouse-deer?

(Tiger lifts off bag and looks around.)

TIGER: Mouse-deer's gone! She tricked me!

STORYTELLER 1: Just then, a man comes walking through the forest. He's picking flowers.

(Man comes in pantomiming picking flowers from trees and shrubs as Storyteller 1 plays xylophone.)

TIGER *(growling)*: Ho, ho, Mouse-deer may fool me, but you won't!

MAN: H-how did Mouse-deer f-fool you?

TIGER: She promised to turn me into two tigers and didn't do it.

MAN (*laughing*): Tiger, there *are* two of you.

TIGER (*looking about*): Two of me? Where?

MAN (*points*): Look in that pool of water over there and you'll see the other tiger.

(*Tiger runs to pool where Mouse-deer drank and stares into it.*)

STORYTELLER 3: When Tiger stares into the still water, he sees himself.

(*Man picks up bag, quickly pantomimes filling it with fruit, and tiptoes out.*)

TIGER: There is another tiger here just like me. Mouse-deer *did* make two out of one. Why, that Mouse-deer is *almost* as clever as I.

(*Tiger goes out, proudly dancing as music ends the scene.*)

ACT 2
MOUSE-DEER AND THE DEEP PIT

Storytellers 1, 2, and 3 sit on one side. Storytellers 4, 5, and 6 sit on other side.

STORYTELLER 1: This story tells how Mouse-deer gets out of a deep pit.

STORYTELLER 2 (*plays bells*): Little Mouse-deer doesn't always look as she walks. Here comes Mouse-deer now, eating a pear and fanning herself with a banana leaf. She does not see the big hole in front of her.

(*Mouse-deer walks across the stage, fanning herself with banana leaf. Suddenly she falls to the floor with a yell, as if falling into a deep pit.*)

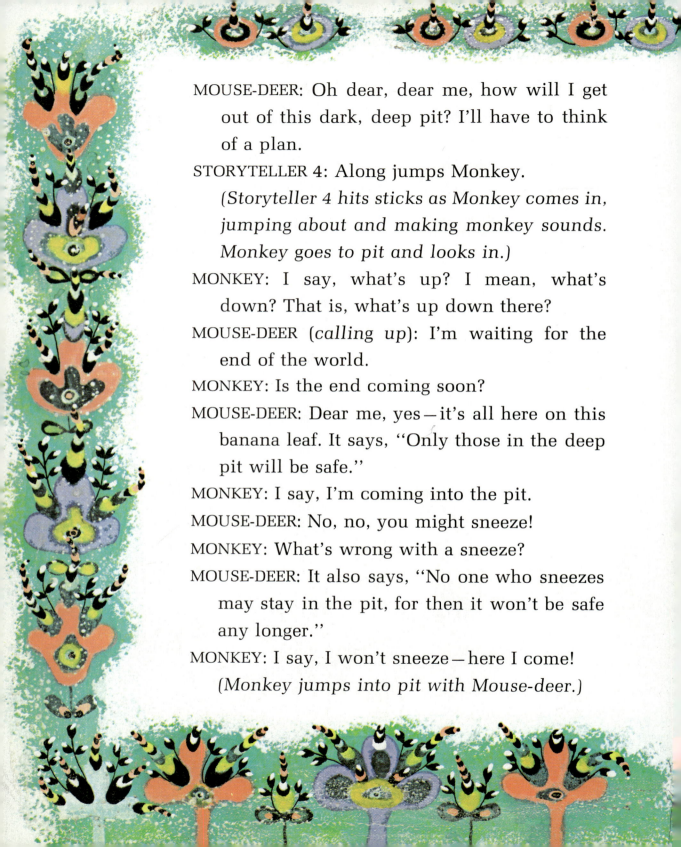

MOUSE-DEER: Oh dear, dear me, how will I get out of this dark, deep pit? I'll have to think of a plan.

STORYTELLER 4: Along jumps Monkey.
(Storyteller 4 hits sticks as Monkey comes in, jumping about and making monkey sounds. Monkey goes to pit and looks in.)

MONKEY: I say, what's up? I mean, what's down? That is, what's up down there?

MOUSE-DEER (calling up): I'm waiting for the end of the world.

MONKEY: Is the end coming soon?

MOUSE-DEER: Dear me, yes—it's all here on this banana leaf. It says, "Only those in the deep pit will be safe."

MONKEY: I say, I'm coming into the pit.

MOUSE-DEER: No, no, you might sneeze!

MONKEY: What's wrong with a sneeze?

MOUSE-DEER: It also says, "No one who sneezes may stay in the pit, for then it won't be safe any longer."

MONKEY: I say, I won't sneeze—here I come!
(Monkey jumps into pit with Mouse-deer.)

STORYTELLER 5: Along comes Elephant.
(Elephant comes in, swinging arms from side to side. Elephant looks down into pit as Storyteller 5 plays gong/drum.)
ELEPHANT: What are you doing down there?
MONKEY: Waiting for the end of the world. Only those in the deep pit will be safe.
ELEPHANT: Well, I'm coming down, too!
MONKEY: No, no, you might sneeze!
ELEPHANT: What's wrong with a sneeze?
MONKEY: No one who sneezes may stay in the pit, for then it won't be safe any longer.
ELEPHANT: Well, *I* won't sneeze. Here I come!
(Elephant jumps into pit.)

STORYTELLER 6: Along comes Boar.

(*Boar comes in, sniffing and pawing the ground. Storyteller 6 plays gong. Boar looks down into pit.*)

BOAR: Sniff. What's happening down there?

MONKEY and ELEPHANT (*together*): We're waiting for the end of the world. Only those in the deep pit will be safe.

BOAR: Then I'm coming down.

MONKEY: No, no, you might sneeze!

BOAR: What's wrong with a sneeze?

ELEPHANT: No one who sneezes may stay in the pit, for then it won't be safe any longer.

BOAR: Then I won't sneeze—here I come!

(*Boar jumps into pit.*)

MOUSE-DEER: Good, we are safe.

STORYTELLER 2: Suddenly Mouse-deer holds her nose.

(*Mouse-deer starts to sneeze.*)

STORYTELLERS 4, 5, and 6 (*together*): The other animals jump back in terror.

MOUSE-DEER: Oh, dear, dear, I'm afraid I'm going to-to-to-

(*Mouse-deer sneezes loudly. Animals scream.*)

MONKEY, ELEPHANT, and BOAR (*together*): Throw Mouse-deer out! Keep the deep pit safe!

(*They throw Mouse-deer out of the pit. Mouse-deer dances about happily.*)

MOUSE-DEER: Monkey, you may wish to read the rest of the banana leaf.

(*Mouse-deer laughs and dances off stage.*)

MONKEY: Let me, let me see that banana leaf!

(*Boar hands him the leaf and Monkey looks at it closely.*)

MONKEY: There is nothing on this leaf!

ELEPHANT: Nothing?

BOAR: Not even one word?

MONKEY: Nothing! Mouse-deer fooled us!

(*The air is filled with the animals' growls as they vainly try to climb up out of the deep pit. At last they stop trying, and from far away all can hear Mouse-deer, laughing. Music ends the play.*)

Skills Lesson: Syllables

Look at the Parts

The band played the song five times. The music sounded good, but in one part someone kept playing the wrong note! The bandleader thought about what he could do.

Then the bandleader had an idea. "Let's break the music down into its parts," he said. "Each person will play his or her part alone."

He listened as each person played, and soon found out who was making the mistake. Then he helped the person play the song the right way.

After that, the band made beautiful music together!

One way to understand something better is to break it into parts. You can do this with words, just as the bandleader did with the music. Then you can work on each part to figure out the word.

The parts of a word are called syllables. You can use these rules to break some words into syllables:

1. If a word has two consonants with one vowel before them and one after them, break the word between the consonants.

2. If a word has a vowel with a consonant and another vowel after it, break after the first vowel. Say the first part, using the long vowel sound. If the sound doesn't make sense, break the word after the consonant. Then say the first part, using the short vowel sound.

3. If a word has a prefix or suffix, break the word between it and the root word.

Read the following story. Use the other words in the sentences and the syllable rules to read the underlined words.

All the people I know <u>overdo</u> things. They tell me <u>unbelievable</u> stories and <u>insist</u> the stories are true. I've heard a hundred <u>incredible</u> tales. Some were so <u>terrifying</u> that my bones shook. Some were so <u>comical</u> that I laughed for days. Can't anyone tell a story without overdoing it?

Read the following sentences and then answer the questions below.

Jan's writing is unreadable.
I spoke to Tom on the telephone.
The car's motor would not start.

1. Which word has three syllables?
2. Which word has four syllables?
3. Which words have two syllables?

Strange As It Seems

The King Who Was *Never* Wrong

Once upon a time a very clever woman named Elsa lived in the land of Baffia. Now, Baffia was ruled by a king named Herbert. He was a good king, but he had one bad habit—never, never, never, would he admit that he might be wrong. "For *I* am the king," he said, "and I'm *always* right."

The people of Baffia loved King Herbert, but they couldn't stand his habit of *always* being right, even when he was wrong. If only someone could show him that he was not *always* right, only *almost* always right!

But who could do this?

Elsa thought that she would take a chance and try, so early one morning she made three drawings and went to the castle.

"I must see the king," Elsa called. "I understand that the king is *always* right, so he may be able to help me with my problems."

By chance King Herbert heard her. Puffing up proudly, he said, "Come in, come in. Of course I'll help you, for I am the king, and I am *never* wrong."

"Oh, thank you," said Elsa. "My problems seem very easy, but I admit freely that *I* cannot answer them."

"Never fear," said King Herbert. "I'll do it for you. Now, what is the first problem?"

"Well," said Elsa, "each night I send my children to their rooms to sleep, but each morning they tell me that they climbed the stairs the whole night long and never got to the top. The walking wearies them so!"

"That's silly," said King Herbert, "for all stairs have to have a top stair."

"I've made a drawing of the stairs," said Elsa. "Would you show me the top stair?"

"I'll do that at once," said King Herbert, taking the drawing from Elsa.

The king stared at it for a long time. At last he frowned and said, "Well, for the very first time in my life, I must say that I've made a mistake. There has to be a top stair, and there isn't. Hmmm, what is your next problem?"

"I have two oxen at home and I have measured them. You see the lines I've made; please tell me — which ox is longer?" said Elsa, giving the king the second drawing.

He looked at her drawing and said, "Why, my dear woman, a child could tell that the one on the top is longer."

"You are the king, and you are always right," said Elsa. "But please, would you be good enough to measure them?"

The king called for a ruler and carefully measured the lines. "Why, they are the same size!" he shouted.

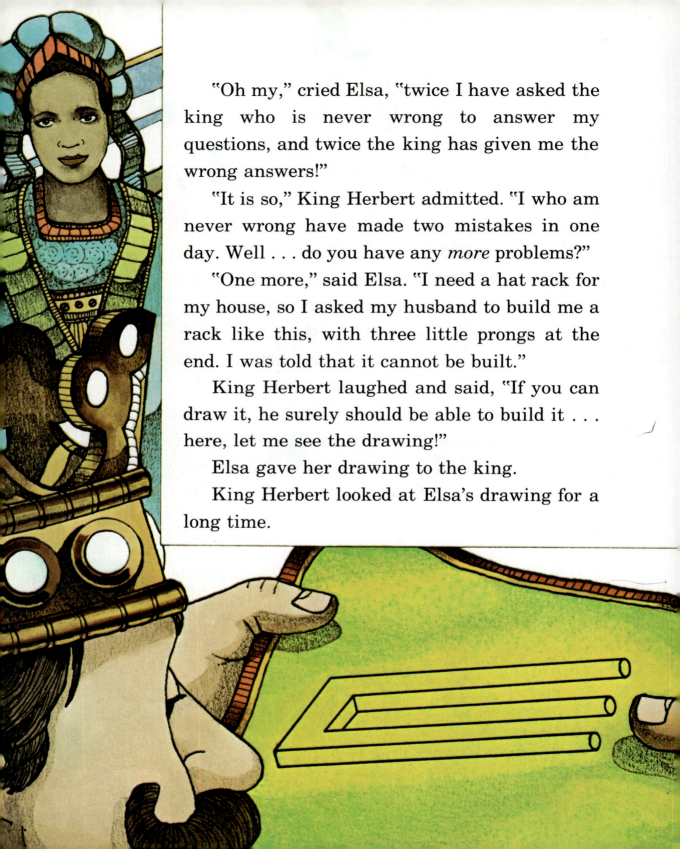

"Oh my," cried Elsa, "twice I have asked the king who is never wrong to answer my questions, and twice the king has given me the wrong answers!"

"It is so," King Herbert admitted. "I who am never wrong have made two mistakes in one day. Well . . . do you have any *more* problems?"

"One more," said Elsa. "I need a hat rack for my house, so I asked my husband to build me a rack like this, with three little prongs at the end. I was told that it cannot be built."

King Herbert laughed and said, "If you can draw it, he surely should be able to build it . . . here, let me see the drawing!"

Elsa gave her drawing to the king.

King Herbert looked at Elsa's drawing for a long time.

At last he said, "Hmmm, you can build the back, and you can build the front . . . but something is *very* strange in the middle."

He stared at her drawing again. At last he handed it back to Elsa. "I was wrong," he admitted. "It cannot be built."

"Oh, my," cried Elsa, "three chances I have given you. And you who are *always* right were wrong three times. I have one more question to ask: Is any person ever right *all* the time?"

The king stared at Elsa. Then suddenly he laughed and said, "Who *indeed* is always right? Not you, not I, not anyone. Thank you, good woman — after this I will think things over and be careful . . . for I, too, can make mistakes."

King Herbert did just that, much to the happiness of the women and men of Baffia. King Herbert kept the drawings Elsa had made, and he spent many hours trying to find the top of those stairs.

Mystery of Oak Island

by DALE TITLER

Every buried treasure has a special story to tell, but no story is stranger than that of the treasure of Oak Island. That treasure is still buried, waiting to be dug up. For almost two hundred years, people have been digging for the treasure. They have never succeeded in finding it; even today no one is sure what is buried on Oak Island.

Discovery

The treasure was first discovered in 1795 when three boys rowed over to Oak Island, a small island just east of Canada. On a hill near the shore, they found a hole. It looked as if the earth had fallen in, after something was buried in the hill. Was it a buried treasure?

The next day the boys returned to the island with shovels and picks and started to dig. Three meters down, they hit something hard — it was a floor of thick wooden boards. Did it cover the treasure? They lifted up the boards: no treasure. Day after day they dug on; at seven meters and ten meters, wooden floors stopped their work again.

Then winter came, and the boys stopped digging. At home they asked about Oak Island and heard some strange stories. Fifty years before, stories said, ships had stopped at the island. One night two fishermen had rowed over to see what was going on. They went on shore and were never seen again. No one was interested in helping the boys dig for treasure on Oak Island.

Some years later a man named John Lynds decided to dig for the treasure. He hired a crew and brought tools to the island. In 1803 the crew began to dig.

As they dug down, they found more wooden floors. At 27 meters they uncovered a new mystery: a large flat stone covered with strange

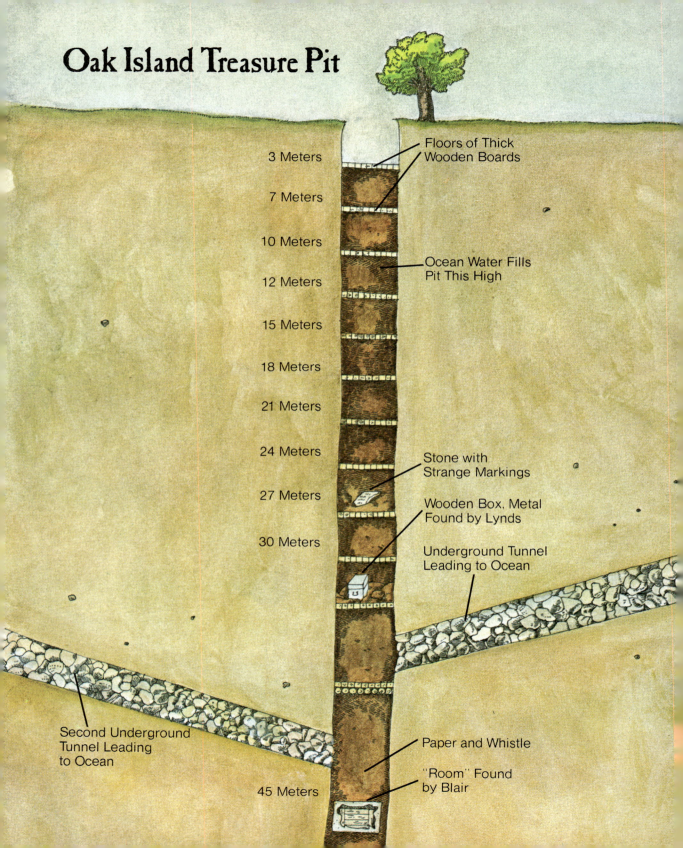

marks. No one could read the words on it.

Thrilled by the discovery of the stone, Lynds's crew went back to work. At 30 meters below the ground, they hit wood. Lynds was sure that the treasure lay just below. Work was stopped until next morning.

But when the crew came back the next day, they found the pit filled with water. They pumped out the water. But the pit filled up again as they pumped it out. Winter came, and all the work stopped.

The next summer Lynds's crew dug a new pit next to the treasure pit. At 33 meters down the second pit, they started to tunnel sideways toward the treasure. As their shovels broke through the last few feet of dirt, a flood of water rushed suddenly into the pit. The crew got away — but now the second pit was filled with water. Lynds gave up the treasure hunt.

Forty years later Lynds tried again. The crew used a drilling machine. At 33 meters they hit a wooden box. When they lifted the drill, they found three pieces of gold on its bit. A shout went up—they had hit the treasure! But it was under 25 meters of water.

Because the water was salty Lynds believed that the people who buried the treasure had dug two tunnels, the second joining the first to the ocean. Ocean water would stop anyone who tried to dig up the treasure.

They soon found the second tunnel. Lynds's crew built a wall to hold the ocean water back, but the pressure of the water quickly knocked the wall down. Lynds dug a new pit, but water quickly filled that pit, too. Lynds gave up again, this time for good.

More People Try

Other people began coming to Oak Island to dig for the treasure. Over the years, they spent more than 70 thousand dollars trying to get at the treasure. They did not succeed.

In 1893 the Oak Island Treasure Company was formed by a man named Blair. Blair opened the first pit again. At 45 meters his drill reached into a "room" two meters deep. The bit brought up such things as a tiny ball of paper with *w* and *i* written on it, and a tiny whistle.

But the pit was still full of ocean water. Blair tried to cut off the water by drilling 50 holes near the ocean. The pit filled up anyway.

Where was the water coming from? The crew forced red dye down into the pit. No dye came out where they thought it would. But red dye showed on the beach at the other side of the island. There was not *one* tunnel guarding the treasure—there were *two* tunnels!

The work went on for four more years. New pits went down, one was as deep as 49 meters. No luck. Finally in 1903 Blair gave up.

Many years later a person named Gilbert Hedden decided to dig up the treasure. He had plenty of money, so he hired a drilling company and used special drilling machines. Hedden worked five years—in vain—and gave up.

Oak Island Today

New people come to Oak Island every summer to dig for the treasure they believe is there. Since the first pit was dug, almost two hundred years ago, over two million dollars have been spent digging more than 40 water-filled shafts on the island. Not one of the more than 20 hard-working crews has been able to dig up the treasure.

What is buried on Oak Island? Why is it buried so well? No one really knows. The people who buried the treasure still hold their secret. The treasure of Oak Island — if there is one — still belongs to them.

Unbelievable Animals

by JAMES MEYERS

Longest-Lived Animals of All

Turtles. The turtle may be one of the slowest animals. But what if it does move slowly? The turtle makes up for it in long life. This cousin of the early dinosaurs lives longer than any other animal on earth! Strange as it may seem, giant turtles have been known to live well over two hundred years. Scientists believe that some turtles may even reach the age of three hundred!

How do these hard-shelled animals live so long? Taking things easy enables them to do it. A turtle eats slowly, moves slowly, and grows slowly. It takes more than a year just for its shell to become hard. And some turtle eggs take as long as a year to hatch!

High Jumpers and Far Travelers

Fleas. Anyone who owns a pet is likely to know all too well a little insect called the flea. These impolite insects live in the hair of many animals. They can go from one animal to another quite easily. But did you know that fleas do not have wings? They cannot fly—but they are wonderful jumpers. They can jump one hundred times their own height. That is the same as a person jumping a 40-story building. Fleas are truly unbelievable jumpers.

Terns. The Arctic tern leads a strange life. It spends three months of each year near the North Pole, three months near the South Pole—and almost six months in the air! This small bird makes one of the longest trips of any animal.

The tern summers in the North. In the fall it heads south. Traveling at 50 to 55 kilometers an hour, stopping to rest and eat on the ocean and on land, the tern flies south for three months. After a trip that may cover 18 thousand kilometers, the tern reaches the South Pole.

But when spring comes, the tern is off again. It makes another 18 thousand-kilometer trip, returning to its home in the North. This little bird, then, flies a round trip covering as much as 36 thousand kilometers. And it repeats the trip each year!

Seals. Alaskan seals are the best long-distance swimmers in the world. In late spring and summer, they bear their young on the rocky islands off Alaska. Then they take to the water. They swim south to avoid the cold of winter. For eight months they stay in the ocean. Sometimes they swim as much as 10 thousand kilometers without once touching land before they return to Alaska in the spring.

Other Unbelievable Animals

The Cheetah. The swiftest person cannot run much faster than 40 kilometers an hour. The fastest dog darts along at 65 kilometers an hour. Racehorses can run from 72 to 80 kilometers an hour. The antelope can fly along the ground at close to one hundred. But no animal can keep up with the swiftest of all the world's runners—the jungle cat known as the cheetah.

Of all the great cats, the cheetah is the swiftest-looking. Its golden coat is covered with black spots. Its legs are longer than the legs of the lion or the tiger. When hunting an antelope, the cheetah can race at 115 kilometers an hour! Once the cheetah decides to attack, there is no animal that can get away from it.

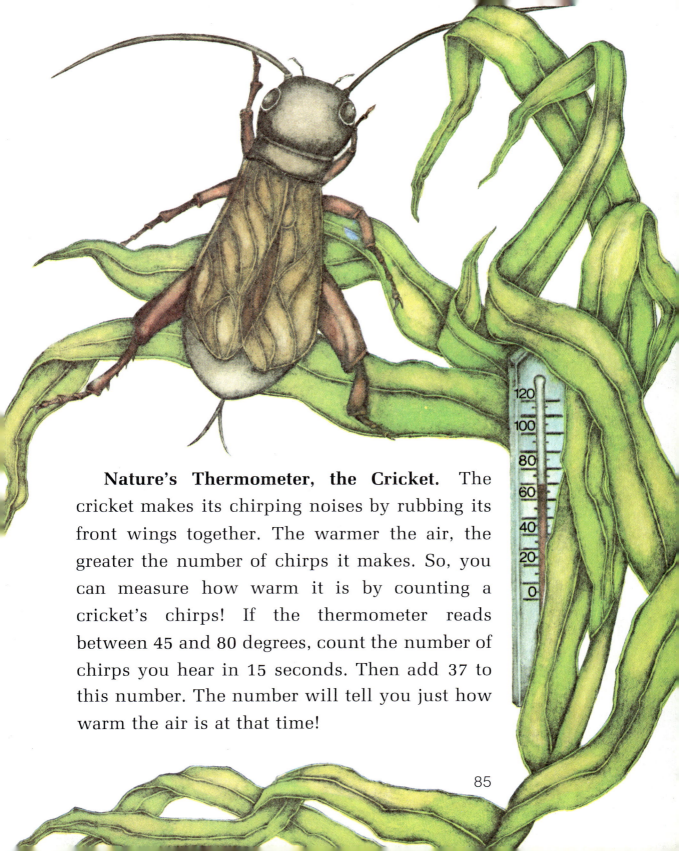

Nature's Thermometer, the Cricket. The cricket makes its chirping noises by rubbing its front wings together. The warmer the air, the greater the number of chirps it makes. So, you can measure how warm it is by counting a cricket's chirps! If the thermometer reads between 45 and 80 degrees, count the number of chirps you hear in 15 seconds. Then add 37 to this number. The number will tell you just how warm the air is at that time!

The Tree Climber. The walking fish has the best of two worlds. In the water it swims like any other fish. But this fish's fins are bent in such a way that they can be used for walking, too. And the walking fish often does take a walk, right out of the water. It climbs the lower branches of trees near the water. This strange fish can live quite well out of water, and even eats insects it finds in the trees.

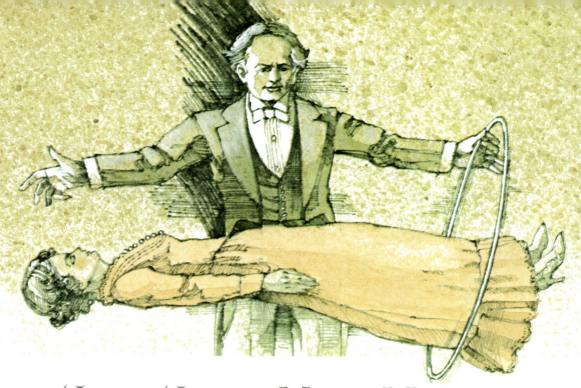

Harry Houdini, Master Magician

Harry Houdini was a great magician—the most amazing magician of his day. He did many things that seemed impossible. People said, "Houdini can do things that no ordinary person can do, so he must have magic powers."

People often want to believe in magic; they want to believe that there are persons who can do the impossible.

Every magician knows this. Magicians make up tricks for people's enjoyment. Magicians smile when people say in amazement, "No, that can't be done . . . you *must* have magical powers!" The magicians know that their tricks have succeeded.

Here are two of the tricks that made Harry Houdini famous . . . and some of the ways he might have done them.

The Man No Locks Could Hold

Houdini was the most famous "escape artist" the world has ever seen. He said, "No jail in the world can hold me; locks are useless against me." And to people's amazement he proved it, time after time. He was locked up in cells in all parts of the world, and he *always* escaped.

Once Houdini was locked up in the strongest cell in Washington, D.C. Everyone was sure that he could never escape from the cell.

Before taking him to the cell, people made very sure that Houdini had not hidden a key on himself. They looked him over very carefully, head to foot. They found no key, so they locked him in the cell and went back to the police chief's office. "We'll wait a while, and then we'll go in and let him out," they said.

The people sat and waited for several minutes. The door opened, and in came Harry Houdini. Not only had he freed himself—he had unlocked all the other cell doors as well!

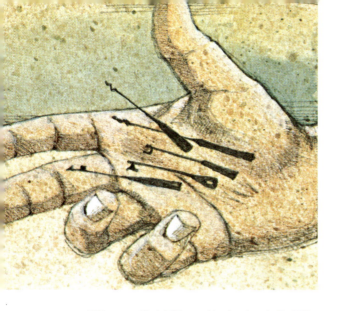

How did Houdini do it? He may have used tiny tools called "picks" to open the locks. For years Houdini had studied books about locks and keys; he bought locks and learned to open them. He could easily open ordinary locks — and to Houdini, most jail locks were ordinary.

Before being locked in a cell, Harry always sent a helper to look over the jail to "see that all was well." The helper told Houdini what kind of locks the jail had. Then it was up to Houdini to get the right kind of pick into the cell. Once that was done he could easily open the cell door and walk out.

This is one way he might have done it. Houdini often knew beforehand what kind of locks the jail had, so when the helper visited the jail, he took along the tiny pick that Houdini needed and let it fall near the cell.

The next day Houdini was carefully searched. Of course, no key was found. But as he was being taken toward the cell, Houdini walked over the pick he needed. He carried it into the cell, stuck to some glue that he had carefully put on his foot.

Escape from the Packing Crate

Another one of Houdini's most amazing tricks used a large packing crate. The crate was put out front where everyone could look as they walked into the show. People saw that the crate was very strong and very well-made, with heavy nails holding the boards together. Houdini said that he would be nailed inside it and would escape without breaking the crate. "Impossible!" people said.

Just before the show started, the packing crate was carried on stage where several people looked the crate over again. At last Houdini climbed inside. The top was put on the crate. Bang, bang, went heavy hammers, driving nails deep into the wooden top. Houdini was inside, and everyone was sure that no one could get out of such a crate.

The curtain closed in front of the crate, loud music played, and people waited. Then suddenly Houdini appeared in front of the curtain, smiling and bowing. The cur-

tain was pulled back. There stood the packing crate, unopened. How had Houdini done it? Had the magician walked right through the wall of the crate?

Houdini may have done the trick this way. Before the crate was carried on stage, he or a helper took all the long nails out of one side of it. Shorter nails were put in their places. The nails were just long enough to fool the people looking over the crate. But

once inside the crate, in back of the curtain, Houdini gave the weak side of the crate several sharp raps. It opened out.

Jumping out, Houdini quickly removed the short nails and hammered the crate closed with large nails. (The hammering could not be heard because of the loud music.) Then Houdini walked out from behind the curtain, smiled, and bowed to the amazed people.

Harry Houdini did his tricks for people's enjoyment; he never said that he had magic powers. But people *did* want to believe. Once Houdini did some of his tricks for a man who had written many famous mystery stories. At the end of the show, Houdini said, "Now, listen. These things seem powerful and impossible. But they are only ordinary tricks. I cannot tell you how I do them, for a magician never gives away his secrets. But really, they are only tricks."

"Oh, no," said the writer, "that cannot be. You *must* have magic powers."

Houdini smiled to himself— he knew that his tricks had succeeded.

Skills Lesson: Topic and Main Idea

Stick to the Topic

Look at the pictures below. Can you tell in one word what each picture shows?

Did you say that the first picture shows a garden, the second a classroom, and the third a fire? If you did, then you told the topic of each picture.

Every story you read has a topic. The topic of a story is what all or most of the sentences are about. You can usually tell the topic in one or two *words*.

Every story also has a main idea. The main idea is the most important point in the story. You can usually tell the main idea in one or two *sentences*.

Read this story and try to figure out the topic and main idea.

Talk about pet cats! Ms. Gold had the most pet cats Tony had ever seen. One day Tony asked Ms. Gold if he could count all her cats. "Well, you can try," she said.

Tony counted 21 cats in the living room. There were 17 cats in the kitchen. Upstairs he found 34 more cats. Tony stopped counting when he reached 80. But he didn't think he'd counted all of them.

Tony said to Ms. Gold, "I don't know how many cats you have, but you have the most cats *I've* ever seen."

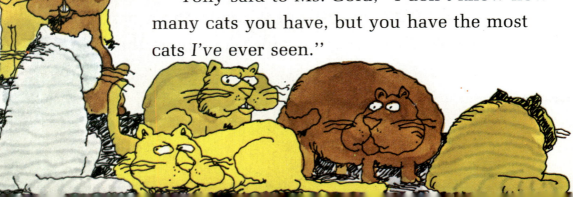

She laughed and said, "The most I've ever seen, too, Tony."

What was the topic of the story? Yes, pet cats. What was the main idea? Ms. Gold had the most pet cats Tony had ever seen.

TRY THIS

What are the topic and main idea of this story?

Pets can be fun, but they can also be lots of trouble. Julie's dog, Rover, usually behaves well. But when Rover sees cats, he acts like a growling tiger.

Bernie has a pet bird named Petey. Petey sings all day long. But sometimes Petey sings all night long, too!

Randy's cat, Dusty, loves to climb. Randy likes to watch Dusty climb along the backyard fence. But when Dusty climbs the old oak tree, Randy has to go to the rescue.

TRY THIS

What was the topic of this lesson? If you said the topic of this lesson was topic and main idea, then you answered correctly.

Tell whether each item listed below is a topic or a main idea. Then tell or write the name of the story in this unit that each topic or main idea describes.

1. Buried treasure.
2. Some animals act in ways that are amazing to people.
3. Tricky pictures.
4. Animals.
5. No one is right all the time.
6. The treasure of Oak Island is still buried and waiting to be dug up.
7. Harry Houdini.
8. Harry Houdini was the most amazing magician of his day.

Look All Around You

Camel Girl

by ELIZABETH COOPER

"If you get up now," shouted Fallah's mother, "you may come with us when we take the camels to the well."

Fallah stood up and stretched. She dressed, ate quickly, and walked out of the tent. Fallah looked around at the desert, which stretched, hot and stony, as far as she could see. Sometimes guests visited Fallah's village; to them the desert seemed an unfriendly place. But to Fallah it just *was* — she and her family had lived in the desert all their lives.

Today was moving day for the village. Several tents were already down, and villagers were beginning to put things on the pack camels. They roped and tied their belongings to camels, making comfortable places for the small children.

This morning Fallah wouldn't help with the packing. Before the village moved, she'd help drive some of the camels to the well. The well was far away, and the camels had not had a drink of water for many days.

Fallah joined her mother, father, brothers, and

sisters, who were readying the camels for the long walk across the desert.

"Don't forget, Fallah, each camel likes to go its own way," said her father. "They have no manners. They can be ghastly beasts. We must keep them together. You'll look after the small, sleepy one and make sure it stays up with us."

With much laughter and shouting, they set out on the long trip over the rough, dry ground.

They walked for hours until the sun stood, hot and white, above them. Much to Fallah's happiness the camels moved along quietly. She knew how impolite and mean and, yes, ghastly camels could be. But her good luck did not last.

They were almost at the well when one of the camels suddenly stopped—it was the very one Fallah was guarding! It broke away from the line and walked slowly to an old, low tree. It got down on its knees, lay down there in the shadow, and closed its eyes.

"Go after the little camel, Fallah," cried her mother.

"Push it, hit it, jump on it," shouted her father. "Make the silly camel move."

Her brother called, "What that camel needs is a hard kick, so give it one, Fallah!"

Fallah ran to the camel, calling, "Don't worry, I'll get it moving. You go on to the well and I'll catch up with you."

As Fallah stood looking down at the sleeping camel, her family moved on, across the desert.

"I know what to do," said Fallah. "I'll speak gently to it." She bent down over her camel and said softly, "Come, rise, my friend. Do you not know that water is near? Are you not thirsty after so many days without water? Do you want all the other camels to drink it up so that there is no water left for you?"

Fallah's camel opened one eye and looked at her; then it went back to sleep.

"It is as they told me," said Fallah. "Camels won't listen to a soft voice." She took a long, deep breath.

"Up, oh idle animal!" Fallah shouted. "Silly, ill-mannered camel, you cannot lie in the sand all day! There is work to be done! We must get the water and hurry back to the village, so get up, you foolish camel!"

The camel opened its eyes and slowly turned its head, looking hard at every part of the desert. At last it looked at Fallah for a long minute. Then the camel made a funny sound, closed its eyes again, and went back to sleep.

"Oh, silly beast!" shouted Fallah. "The well will be dry before we get there!"

She leaned down, got a good hold on the camel's harness, and began to pull. She pulled hard, but she could not get the camel to its feet.

Then Fallah tickled the camel's head. The head swung up and gave her a hard thump. It knocked Fallah flat on the sand.

Fallah sat there, thinking. What if the camel *never* got up? Maybe the camel would still be there, sleeping in the sand, when Fallah's family came back from the well. "Impossible camel," muttered Fallah, "you would rather sleep than drink cool water."

WATER—maybe that was the thing! Fallah took a piece of cloth, wet it with water from her water bag, and splashed a little on the camel's nose. Then she held out the wet cloth.

The camel got a sniff of the water; in a second it was on its feet.

At first Fallah did not walk fast. It was hard to walk backwards holding the wet cloth in front of the camel's nose.

But as the camel moved faster, so did Fallah. At last Fallah turned and ran, with the camel close behind her.

"Yes," shouted Fallah happily, "race with me, oh camel, and we shall soon be at the well."

In a short time the girl and camel were racing down the last low hill near the well. When the camel smelled the well water, it turned away from Fallah and ran to join the other camels already drinking at the well.

As to Fallah, she was out of breath and very warm. She walked slowly over to her family. As she came near them, she heard their cheers and laughter.

"Many a camel driver have I known," said her father. "Some were fast, and some were slow." He laughed. "But you, Fallah — you are the fastest camel driver of all."

(To be read by the teacher.)

Poems by Children

Dragonfly

Dragonfly, Dragonfly,
Come over the river by and by;
On the eastern bank they are
 beating a drum,
On the western bank they are striking
 a gong.

from HONG KONG

Bon Voyage

With one half of a newspaper
I made a little boat,
And in the fountain of my home
It's nice to see it float.

My sister with her paper fan
Blows and blows on it.
Bon Voyage! Bon Voyage!
Little paper ship.

from MEXICO

Fur Traders Descending the Missouri,
by George Caleb Bingham

Art Around the World

People all over the world have art. Art is an important part of people's lives today, and it has been from very early times. Artists have always sought to share their thoughts and feelings through their work. Using paints and chalks, wood and metal, they often succeed better than they could with words.

Artists often show the people, places, and ways of living that are familiar to them. They record their worlds in works of art. Through their eyes we can see worlds that have long since passed away. We can understand ways of life that are very different from our own.

This drawing was done by an Eskimo artist. Look at it carefully. What does it tell you about Eskimo life? The drawing is simple, with strong lines and shapes. It was made by cutting lines into a stone; the picture was then printed from the stone.

Hunters at the Floe Edge, **by Enooky**

The Fruit Stall, **by Olga Costa**

The Fruit Stall, painted by an artist from Mexico, shows several straw baskets overflowing with delicious fruit. The rich ripe colors make the fruit stall look very inviting. Do you have the same kind of fruit where you live?

Bom Bosh was king of Bushongo, a country in Africa, more than three hundred years ago. Here is his likeness carved in wood. Look at the square shapes of Bom Bosh's headdress and seat, and the smooth, rounded shapes of his face and body.

Royal Portrait of Bom Bosh

Project for a Family Group, **by Henry Moore**

This family group in metal, by a British artist, could really be from any part of the world. Do you see how each person in the family is touching another? Their arms almost form a circle. What feeling has the artist sought to give about the family?

Landscape in Spring, by Rasic

Artists often enjoy drawing pictures of the countryside. On this page is a happy country scene from Yugoslavia, filled with bright colors and large and small shapes. Each branch of every tree is shown. Why do you think the artist did that?

Here you see a picture painted in Japan, a country halfway around the world. This scene is part of a longer painting made more than five hundred years ago. Do you like the darkish colors which the artist used?

All around the world people eat and sleep and play and study. The art of each place mirrors what the artists see around them. That is why a work of art tells us something about the time and place where it was made.

Long Landscape Scroll, **by Sesshū**

Robin and the Sled Dog Race

by SARA MACHETANZ

Robin walked through the snow, carefully carrying a pan of fish soup to the pole where Nubbin was chained.

Then she carried pans to Flip and Flop.

The sled dogs did not touch the food. Their eyes followed Robin, but they sat straight and still. Only their tails moved, making nests in the snow behind them.

"All right," Robin said—and three black noses darted into three pans.

The soup was made from fish Robin had helped catch in the summer. Robin hoped it would make her dogs run fast. Tomorrow was the final "three dogger" race at the Alaska Snow Fair. And Mark Woods's time was two minutes and ten seconds better than Robin's.

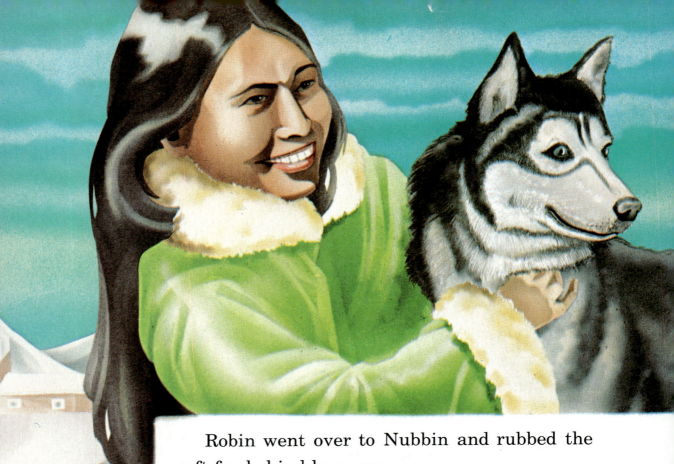

Robin went over to Nubbin and rubbed the soft fur behind her ears.

"You're the best leader in all the world," she told Nubbin. "Tomorrow we'll more than make up the time we're behind."

Then she looked closely at Nubbin's paws to see if there were any cuts—they were fine. She looked at Flip's and Flop's paws and they were fine, too.

As Robin looked over her dogs, she thought about the months she had worked to make them a team. She thought back to when they were small and followed along beside a team of grown dogs.

She remembered the first times they had been put in harness—Nubbin beside a leader. That was the way they had learned to go right when she called "gee" and to go left when she called "haw."

Robin had wanted a team that obeyed, so she had worked hard to teach them to follow commands. And she had toughened them up with runs to the mailbox three kilometers away every day.

"Time to eat, Robin." Her mother stood in the door, the lamp shining gold behind her.

Robin jumped to her feet. "I'll be right in," she answered.

On her way to the house, she picked up an armful of wood. She'd been so busy with her dogs she hadn't even thought of wood to fill the woodbox. In the house Robin put the wood in the box and said, "I'm hungry!"

"So am I," said her father, coming to the table. "How are your dogs, Robin?"

"Fine," Robin said. "They're eating well and their paws aren't cracked at all, so I'm sure they can make up the time we're behind."

"Mark's dogs are larger than yours," said her father.

"I know," Robin said, "but that doesn't mean they're the best. My team follows commands better than his."

"That's very true, Robin." Her mother came over and patted Robin's hair. "We just don't want you to be too unhappy if you don't win."

"My team'll make up that time," Robin said. "They'll win tomorrow."

The next morning Robin climbed out of bed before the fire was made.

"You must be trying to make up that time right now," her father said.

"I just wanted to get up early," Robin said, laughing. "I'll light the fire." But really, Robin hadn't been able to sleep; now she was so excited she couldn't even finish eating.

The dogs were excited, too. When Robin and her father went out for them, they barked and howled and then ran in circles and dug at the ground. They pulled hard on their collars as Robin pulled them toward the truck. Their front feet lifted up from the ground and they danced along on their back legs.

On the drive to the Snow Fair, the dogs quieted down. They curled themselves up like snail shells and went to sleep. But when Robin's father parked in the field beside the Fair, they woke up.

Other teams were barking and the dogs grew more excited than ever. They pulled against their chains and barked back.

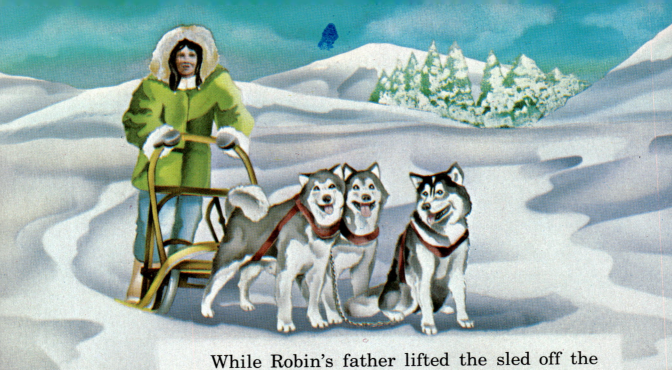

While Robin's father lifted the sled off the top of the truck, Robin laid out the harnesses. She unchained Nubbin and out she jumped.

"Whoa, Nubbin, easy, girl, easy," said Robin, holding Nubbin and slipping on her harness. Once in harness Nubbin stood still while Robin harnessed Flip and Flop. Then — her father holding Nubbin tightly and Robin riding the sled — they brought the dogs to their place behind Mark Woods's team.

Mark's dogs were ready to go, too; Mark and his keeper could hardly hold them while the timer counted off the seconds. At the count of "one" Mark's team was off.

After a two-minute wait, it would be time for Robin's team to go.

Father looked back at Robin. "Just catch up to Mark, and you've made up two minutes. Then you have only ten seconds to go. Good luck, Robin!"

The timer began to count, "One minute, thirty seconds," and Robin suddenly heard sled dogs barking behind her.

"Thirty seconds . . . Twenty seconds . . ."

Then Robin heard nothing but the counting.

"Five, four, three, two, one!"

"Let's go!" Robin shouted. Nubbin and the team shot ahead.

Robin started out running behind the sled. When she was out of breath, she jumped on the runners where she stood on one foot and pushed with the other. As soon as she caught her breath, she jumped off to run again.

Uphill, downhill, over snow and ice, and across roads that were closed to traffic, Robin ran and raced her team. When she came to the pine forest that was just halfway on the five kilometer course, Robin could hardly believe it. She didn't feel at all tired.

But Robin was worried. She was pushing her team more than she ever had. And still she had not caught up with Mark.

"Run, Nubbin, run, run, run," she urged. Up the steepest hill Robin pushed until she was panting as hard as the dogs. And then, just over the top, she saw something that made her hold onto her sled and catch her breath.

At the foot of the hill were Mark and his team. But they weren't running straight ahead. They were turning left into the bushes. Robin could hear the dogs barking and Mark yelling. She saw Mark jump off his sled, turn it over, and run to his lead dog. Then Robin saw why the dogs had turned off-trail. In the bushes stood a large moose.

Nubbin, Flip, and Flop caught sight of the dogs and the moose at the same second Robin did. All at once, all together, they shot ahead, flying down the hill. Flip and Flop began to bark wildly and Nubbin's ears and tail went straight up. At the place where Mark's dogs had turned off, Nubbin began to go left, too.

"Gee, Nubbin," Robin yelled. "Gee!"

Hearing Robin's voice, Nubbin turned back on-trail again. Not Flip and Flop. They pulled towards the moose with all their might, and Robin knew they would finally pull Nubbin along with them.

"Gee, Flip, gee, Flop," she shouted.

Flip slowed down.

"Gee," Robin urged, "gee, gee, gee!"

At that Flip pulled back in line and Flop, feeling the pull on the harness, followed.

"Whew!" Robin said loudly as she passed Mark's team.

Robin saw that Mark was having problems, for his dogs seemed to be tangled in their harnesses.

Here's my chance, Robin thought. "Let's go, Nubbin," she sang out. Then suddenly she had another thought. The moose might go after Mark and his dogs; it could hurt them.

Once Robin thought of that, she knew she had to send help back to Mark, even if she lost several seconds—even if she lost the race.

Robin saw four men watching the race and called "Whoa" to Nubbin.

Nubbin turned her head. "Stop," she seemed to ask, "when the finish line is ahead?"

"Whoa," Robin called again, and then she said to the men, "Mark Woods's team went after a moose and got tangled up."

"We'd better go help him," one man said, starting to hurry down the trail.

"Wait," another shouted after him, "here comes Mark now." He turned toward Robin and said, "Get going, girl!"

But Robin was already going.

"Run, Nubbin, run," Robin shouted. She jumped off the sled and ran until she could run no longer. When she jumped on again, she turned for a quick look and saw that Mark was getting closer!

"Faster, Nubbin, faster," Robin cried as she came to the home stretch.

She didn't look back again, but she knew Mark was close because she could hear him calling to his team. Any second she thought that Mark would call "trail" and she would have to pull over.

Up ahead Robin saw the crowd at the finish line and heard them cheering and yelling.

Then she heard the announcer's voice boom out, "Here they come now . . . it's Robin Stone and Mark Woods. The teams are very close, but Robin Stone is in the lead. Now Robin is crossing the finish line . . . this will be a close one . . . Mark Woods is coming up fast . . . Mark is over. . . ."

Robin stopped her sled and leaned across it, trying to catch her breath. She had crossed first, but had she made up the time needed to beat Mark? The announcer didn't say. He was calling off the other teams.

Nubbin was panting so hard she shook. Robin went to her, dropped to her knees, and put her arm around Nubbin.

"You are the best leader in all the world," she told her. "And you are the best team," she said to Flip and Flop, "even if we don't win."

"Robin!" She heard her father's excited voice. "Robin, you won by just two seconds!" Robin's father hugged her. "The best trained team turned out to be the best team after all, didn't it?" he said.

Robin felt warm all over. "Sure did," she said . . . for that was something she'd believed since her first "gee" and "haw."

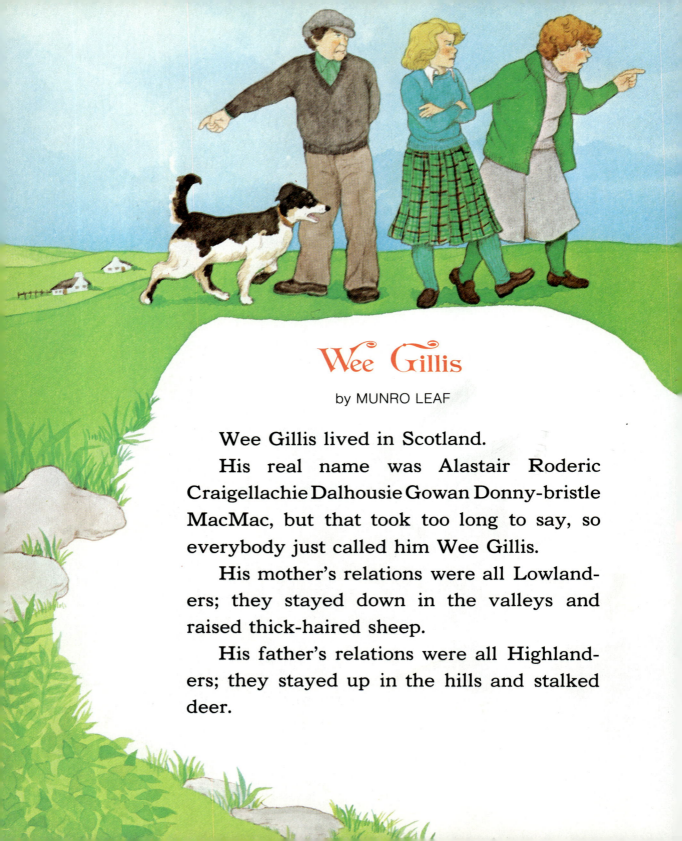

Wee Gillis

by MUNRO LEAF

Wee Gillis lived in Scotland.

His real name was Alastair Roderic Craigellachie Dalhousie Gowan Donny-bristle MacMac, but that took too long to say, so everybody just called him Wee Gillis.

His mother's relations were all Lowlanders; they stayed down in the valleys and raised thick-haired sheep.

His father's relations were all Highlanders; they stayed up in the hills and stalked deer.

Wee Gillis didn't know which he wanted to be, a Lowlander or a Highlander.

His mother's relations all thought that his father's relations were very foolish to run and climb and creep around the hills stalking deer. His father's relations all thought that his mother's relations were very silly to drive and call their long-haired sheep.

Wee Gillis didn't know, but he watched them both and he was cheerful and friendly.

So for one year he went to live in the Lowlands with his mother's relations. Every day he rose early and ate, and then set out with the long-haired sheep along the valleys. At night he called and called them, and brought them home again.

Once he was late in getting them home. Then the relations all asked him what had kept him. He had to tell them that the sheep wouldn't come when he called. Then the relations all said that he didn't shout loud enough. The sheep couldn't hear him through the heavy mist.

So every night when the mists would come down over the valleys, Wee Gillis would shout a little louder than he had before. That was fine for his lungs — by the end of the year they were very, very, very strong.

On the first day of the new year, Wee Gillis went up into the Highlands.

Every day he rose early and ate with his father's relations. Then he set out walking and crawling, running and creeping all over

the hills stalking deer. He would hide behind bushes and sit on the low grass. Sometimes he would have to be quiet for hours at a time. You would have thought that he was a stone.

Once, while he was stalking, he sighed a big sigh because he had stayed still for so long. The noise that it made scared a deer so that it ran away.

Then the relations all told Wee Gillis that he didn't keep quiet enough. He must learn to hold his breath.

So day after day, sitting among the bushes and on the low grass, Wee Gillis would hold his breath longer and longer, to keep from sighing so he wouldn't scare the deer. That was fine for his lungs—by the end of the year they were very, very strong.

So year in and year out, Wee Gillis would take turns calling the sheep in the Lowlands and stalking the deer in the Highlands—and all the while his lungs grew stronger and stronger.

At last the day came when he must decide for all time: Which was he to be?

A Lowlander who called sheep?

Or a Highlander who stalked deer?

Bright and early in the morning, there were two loud knocks on his door. When he opened it, there stood his Uncle Andrew from the Lowlands and his Uncle Angus from the Highlands.

Gillis dressed in a hurry, and away they went, out into the morning. They walked and walked, not saying a word, down through the valleys and up over the hills until at last they found just the right spot for deciding. Then his Uncle Andrew and his Uncle Angus stopped and stood very still. They turned to Wee Gillis.

He was just halfway up the side of a middle-sized hill. He was not in the Lowlands and not in the Highlands, just in the middle. And there he had to choose for all time.

Gillis looked down and looked up, and then he looked at his uncles and they began to talk. First they pleaded, and then they begged very softly and very quietly, one at a time. They politely waited for each to finish what he had to say before the other began. But still Wee Gillis could not decide.

So the uncles' voices grew louder and louder. They didn't wait for each other to finish talking any more. They shouted and screamed and yelled until they jumped up and down and stamped their feet. You could hear them shouting all the way down in the valleys and all the way up in the hills.

Suddenly his uncles stopped jumping and shouting. A very large man had come up behind them. He was carrying something brown and big, but he put it down beside a rock and then he looked at Wee Gillis and then at Uncle Andrew and then at Uncle Angus. When they were very quiet, he sat down on a rock.

He picked up the big brown thing that looked like a bag with sticks on it. He took a deep breath and puffed his cheeks. He shut his eyes and blew into one end of it with all his might, but — nothing happened. He shook his head sadly and tried again, but nothing happened.

And then he was very sad and he said so. He was almost ready to cry. He was a bagpiper, and he had just made these fine new bagpipes to play on, but he had made them too big. And he didn't have breath enough to blow them.

Uncle Andrew was sorry for him, so he tried to blow them, but he couldn't. Uncle Angus was sorry for him too, so he tried to blow them, but he couldn't. So they all sat down on rocks and were sad together.

Wee Gillis wished that his uncles would ask him to try. But they didn't, so he just stood and looked as though he would like to. After a long time the large man saw him and shook his head slowly. But because Wee Gillis looked so wanting-to, the large man asked him if he would like to try.

Wee Gillis said, "Aye," so he did.

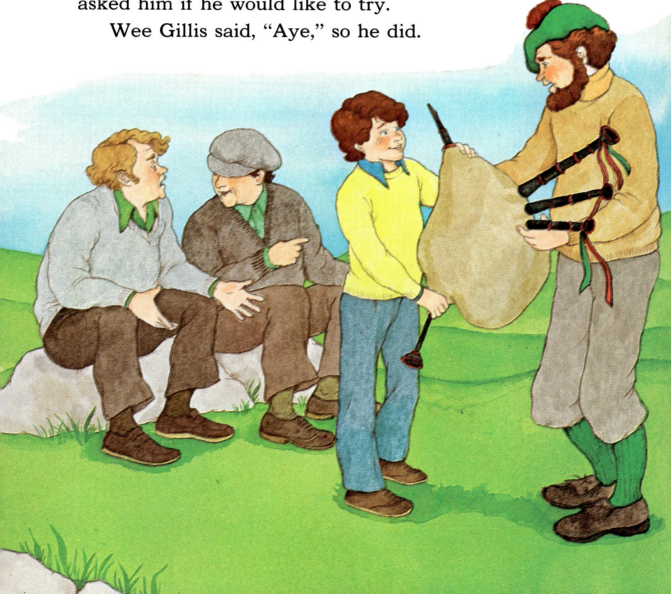

First he took a deep breath the way he used to when he was going to call the sheep on a misty night in the Lowlands. Then he held it the way he used to when he was sitting very still stalking deer in the Highlands. And then he BLEW with all the force in his very, very strong lungs.

The bag filled up and let out a screech through every one of its pipes. And the large man and Uncle Andrew and Uncle Angus fell off their rocks with surprise.

So the large man taught him how to make music. Now Wee Gillis is welcome down in the Lowlands and up in the Highlands. But most of the time he just stays in his house halfway up the side of a middle-sized hill and plays THE BIGGEST BAGPIPES IN ALL SCOTLAND.

(To be read by the teacher.)

The Piper Came to Our Town

The piper came to our town,
To our town, to our town,
The piper came to our town,
And he played bonnily.

He played a tune the lord to please,
A tune brought new from o'er the seas,

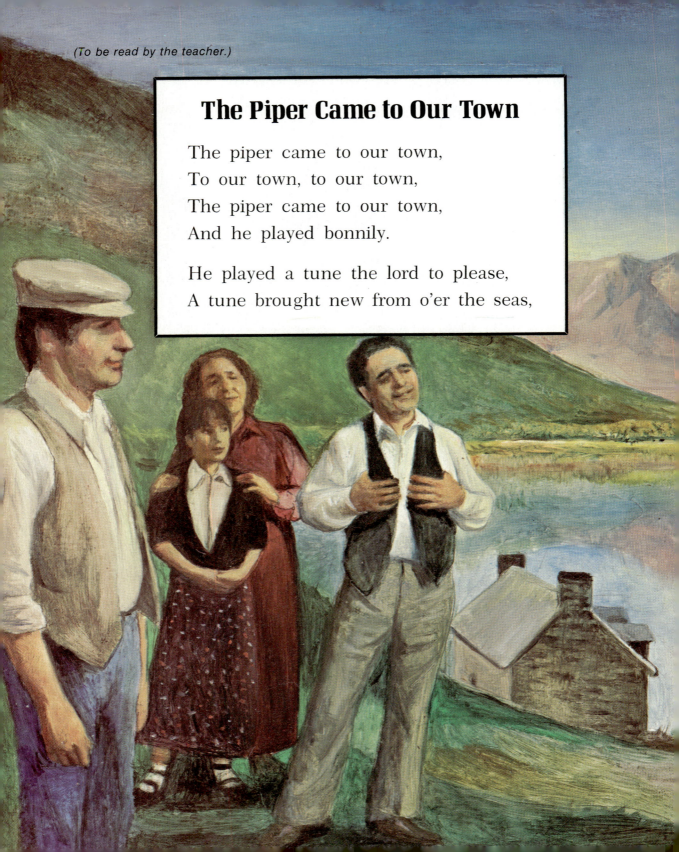

And then he gave his bags a squeeze,
And played another key.

And wasn't he a fine man,
A fine man, a fine man?
And wasn't he a fine man,
The piper of Dundee?

TRADITIONAL SCOTTISH SONG

Taro and the Tofu

by MASAKO MATSUNO

It was windy, and the wind was cold. The cold, windy day was growing into a cold, windy night. From the window Taro could see the evening star already shining brightly in the east. Taro was watching for the tofu seller.

In Japan *tofu* is what we call "bean curd"—it is very delicious, and it is one of the most important foods of that country.

Taro's mother bought tofu from a man who came along the street every evening. But on this cold, windy evening, the man did not come.

In their warm house Taro and his mother waited and waited until finally it was time to cook supper.

"I wonder what has happened to him," said Taro's mother. "This is the first time he hasn't come without letting us know."

"Shall I run to his shop?" asked Taro.

His mother was unsure. "It's getting dark . . . and cold, too."

"That's all right," said Taro, "it's not so late yet, is it? I'll get the tofu for you, Mother."

From beyond the woods the cold wind blew. Taro, holding a small pan for tofu in one hand and a silver coin in the other, began running as soon as he left the house.

The shopping street was crowded with people buying good food for supper. The shops were light and cheerful.

"Come in and buy, come in and buy! My fish are delicious!" a loud voice called from one of the fish stores.

But Taro didn't stop—this wasn't the place he was looking for. He ran in the direction of the man's shop which was at the end of the

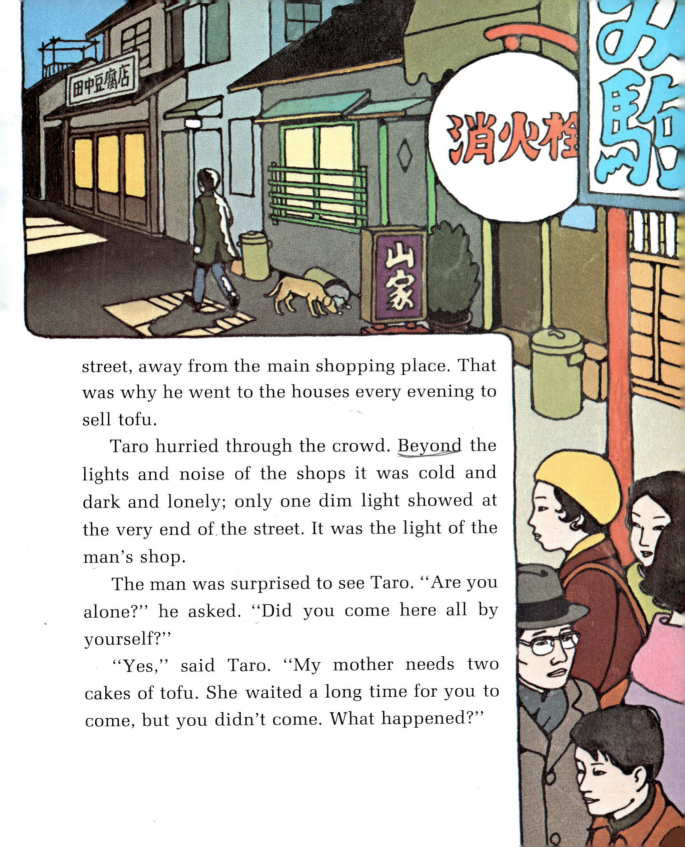

street, away from the main shopping place. That was why he went to the houses every evening to sell tofu.

Taro hurried through the crowd. <u>Beyond</u> the lights and noise of the shops it was cold and dark and lonely; only one dim light showed at the very end of the street. It was the light of the man's shop.

The man was surprised to see Taro. "Are you alone?" he asked. "Did you come here all by yourself?"

"Yes," said Taro. "My mother needs two cakes of tofu. She waited a long time for you to come, but you didn't come. What happened?"

The man took the tofu pan from Taro and said, "I'm sorry, but my grandson doesn't feel well today, so I couldn't leave him alone. But I'll come to your house tomorrow evening," the man added. He handed Taro the filled tofu pan, saying, "Then you won't have to come down in the cold."

"How much?" asked Taro.

"Thirty yen."

Taro handed the coin to the man, who slowly counted out the change under the dim light of the shop.

"Thank you, Taro," he said. "You'd better hurry home, for your mother must be waiting for you."

"Yes — good-by!"

"Don't run, Taro!" the man shouted after him. "My tofu is soft. Carry it carefully so it doesn't break!"

Taro did not run, but he walked fast. Whenever Taro did an errand, his mother let him keep ten yen for himself, so he was in a hurry to get to the little candy store on the main shopping street.

The candy store was run by a lady with big glasses. She always sat in a far corner of the shop, reading a newspaper. She rarely said more than a few words to people. "Thank you, good boy," or "Thank you, good girl," she would say, never looking up from her paper. It was one of the seven wonders to Taro how she knew a boy was a boy — or a girl a girl — without ever looking at them.

And the lady never seemed to care if the children took a long time to decide what to buy with their pocket money. It made Taro feel that all the candies in the store belonged to him until at last he decided just what to buy.

Taro had to decide quickly today so he could hurry home with the tofu.

Two boxes of chocolate, he said to himself, putting his hand in his pocket for the change the man had given him. Taro picked one of the coins to give to the lady.

But, wait, it was a 50-yen coin!

Where did I get this?

Taro looked at the coin in surprise.

"I thought the man gave me seven 10-yen coins, for the tofu was thirty yen, and I gave him a 100-yen coin," thought Taro. "One, two, three, four, five, six . . . Here are six 10-yen coins and a 50-yen . . . Then the man made a mistake. I must return the extra forty yen to him right away. He will be sorry if he finds that he lost money."

But outside it was already dark and the wind was very cold.

"It's getting late, and very cold . . ." a strange little voice whispered inside Taro's head. "Why not tomorrow? Even if the man worries, the mistake is his own fault. It's very cold, and

Mother must be waiting," the secret voice said.

Taro looked at the money in his hand and then at the cold outdoors. "It's just the same if you give the money back tomorrow," whispered the voice again. "Besides, who knows that you've got the money? No one need know. Just think, with forty yen to spend, you could buy sweet beans and salted beans and chocolate and even more . . . Right?"

"Oh, no—" it was almost a shout inside him—"No, no, it's not right. This is not my money. It belongs to the man, even if it was his fault that he gave me the wrong change. I don't want the candies!" Taro was talking to himself very fast now, as if he were in a hurry to rid himself of the strange, secret voice inside his head. "I will return the money right now."

Taro called to the lady of the candy store, but his voice sounded so dry and cracked that only a little low whisper came out.

"I'll take two boxes of chocolate candy today," he said.

"Thank you, good boy," answered the lady without looking up.

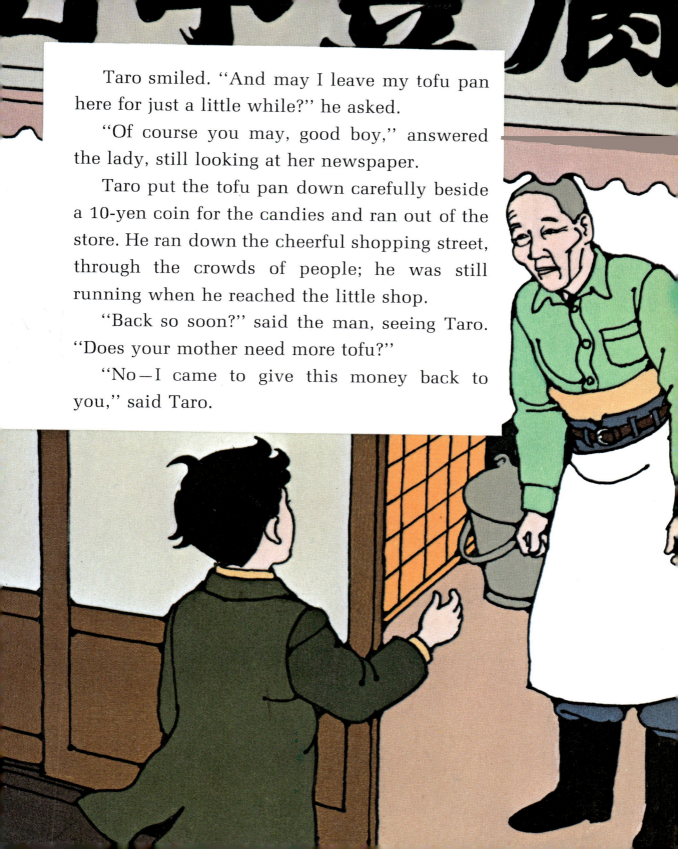

Taro smiled. "And may I leave my tofu pan here for just a little while?" he asked.

"Of course you may, good boy," answered the lady, still looking at her newspaper.

Taro put the tofu pan down carefully beside a 10-yen coin for the candies and ran out of the store. He ran down the cheerful shopping street, through the crowds of people; he was still running when he reached the little shop.

"Back so soon?" said the man, seeing Taro. "Does your mother need more tofu?"

"No—I came to give this money back to you," said Taro.

"What money?"

"You gave me the wrong change; you gave me forty extra yen."

"Really? I didn't even see it. Are you sure the money isn't yours?"

"Yes," said Taro, "I'm sure that you gave me a 50-yen coin for a 10-yen coin. I'll put the money here, all right? I must hurry because Mother is waiting for me."

"Thank you very much, Taro," said the man with gladness in his face.

Taro was happy, but he felt shy too, for he remembered the strange little voice.

"Not at all," he said quickly. Before he knew it he found himself taking one of the boxes of chocolate candy from his pocket. "For your grandson," he said.

"Thank you . . . thank you . . ."

The lady in the candy store was still reading her newspaper when Taro stopped to pick up the tofu pan.

"Thank you for keeping it for me," said Taro.

"Not at all, good boy," said the lady, and much to Taro's surprise, she looked up, straight at him.

Taro had never seen her look at anything but her newspaper. What was more, she was smiling at him—it was almost as if she knew what had happened—but, no, it couldn't be!

"You'd better hurry, good boy. It's very late," said the lady.

Taro nodded and went out of the store with his tofu pan.

Most of the shops on the shopping street were closed now, and only a few people were still there. The wind was very cold.

Anyway, thought Taro, I don't really care if the lady knows what the voice said, because I gave back the money.

He was so happy that he wanted to run all the way home, but he remembered to walk carefully with the tofu. His hands ached with the cold by the time he got there.

At home Taro told his mother and father what had happened to make him so late. He told them about finding the extra forty yen, and he told them about returning to the man's shop. He told them everything—but he didn't tell them about the strange, secret voice in his head, and he did not tell them about giving the candy to the man's sick grandson. Why? Taro just felt like keeping those things to himself.

157

"May I have a candy now?" he asked.

"Yes, but just one. Supper is almost ready," said his mother.

It was still windy outside, and the wind was very cold.

But Taro felt warm. And the chocolate candy was very good.

Skills Lesson: Reading Maps

A Key to Reading Maps

A map is a drawing of a place. It can show an area as small as your neighborhood or as large as the world. A map gives you information about an area by showing many different details.

A map key explains the symbols you see on the map.

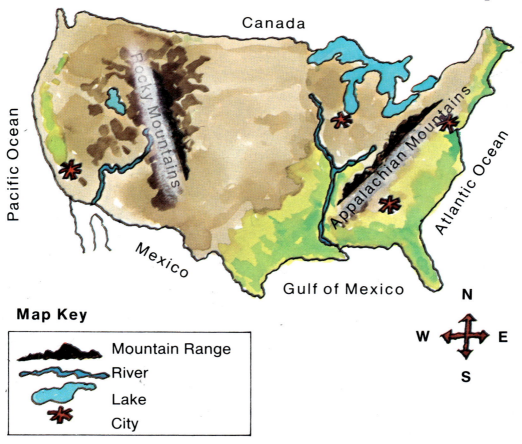

Below are some facts about some of the places on the map. Use the map key to find these places on the map.

1. The Great Lakes make up the largest group of lakes in the country.

2. Strong winds blow from Lake Michigan, one of the Great Lakes, across the city of Chicago. That is why Chicago is known as "The Windy City."

3. The Colorado River is in the western United States.

4. The Mississippi River flows from north to south. It is the largest river in our country.

Use the words *north*, *south*, *east*, or *west* to tell where these places are on the map:

Rocky Mountains   Atlantic Ocean
Gulf of Mexico   Canada

Explorers

The Story of Christopher Columbus

by ANN McGOVERN

Christopher Columbus lived in the 1400's. He had a dream. He wanted to sail west, across the unknown ocean, to India. After many years the rulers of Spain gave him three ships to try out this idea.

Sailing the Sea of Darkness

Three wooden ships were ready. It would take a crew of ninety sailors to sail them. But who would want to sail over an unknown ocean? Many sailors thought the world was flat; they did not want to sail until they fell off the rim of the world.

How could Columbus get sailors for his ships? The King's soldiers forced some people to sign up. He got other people from the town jail. They'd been forced to make a choice: They could stay in jail or they could sail with Columbus. They decided to take a chance with Columbus.

Some of the crew were young men looking for adventure. Some were old sailors looking for gold. Columbus made sure he had trained men, too. There were doctors and able sailors.

At last everything was ready.

On board was a trunk piled full of things for trading—glass beads and red caps, rings and bells. There was food enough to last a year, and there was enough water to drink.

On the third day of August, in the year 1492, Christopher Columbus set sail from Spain. Three small wooden ships—the Niña, the Pinta, and the Santa María—sailed out to journey over an unknown sea.

"Turn Back! Turn Back!"

Columbus kept a log of the voyage. Each day he wrote how far they had sailed, what had been seen, and what had happened.

On the third day at sea, there was trouble with the steering on the Pinta. They had to stop at a nearby island to fix it.

They sailed on, but they were still in sight of land. On September 6 the crew saw fire and smoke rising from the top of a tall mountain. They were so scared by it that they wanted to turn back at once. Quietly, in a sure voice, Columbus told them there was nothing to fear.

By September 9 they had sailed out of sight of land. For days they sailed; for weeks they sailed. Never before had they sailed so long without seeing land.

Most of the sailors grew afraid, surrounded Columbus, and begged, "Turn back, quickly, before the sea dragons eat us."

But Columbus was not afraid, for he knew there were no sea dragons.

He tried to cheer up the crew by talking about the gold that would soon belong to them.

He told them the King would give money to the first person who saw land.

But the sailors muttered and complained. The crew complained when the wind blew too hard, and they complained when there was no wind at all. And they complained about the weeds they saw in the sea.

"Many bunches of very green weeds," Columbus wrote in the log on September 16.

Some of the sailors were afraid the ships would get stuck in the thick green and yellow weeds. Columbus said the ships would sail right through. And they did.

On the night of September 25, a shout came from the Pinta. "Land ahoy! Land ahoy! The reward is mine!"

Everyone shouted that they saw land. Columbus fell to his knees in thanks.

That night no one went to sleep, but when the morning came, there was no land in sight.

What they'd thought to be land had been only a low cloud. Columbus wrote in the log that what they had guessed to be land was nothing but sky.

That day the crew became angrier than ever. They muttered, "There's not much drinking water left. We will die of thirst. Let's throw Columbus overboard. We'll say he slipped and fell into the ocean."

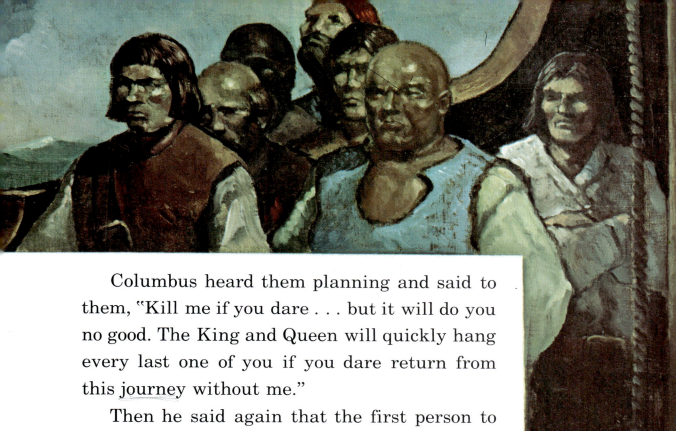

Columbus heard them planning and said to them, "Kill me if you dare . . . but it will do you no good. The King and Queen will quickly hang every last one of you if you dare return from this journey without me."

Then he said again that the first person to sight land would get a reward. "And I myself promise to give that person a fine coat of silk," he said.

But these words did not comfort the crew. They kept a close watch on Columbus, still ready to kill him.

Columbus thought, "Land is near, I'm sure of it. But how can I make my crew believe it?"

He told them, "Allow me three more days. Only three days. If we do not see land by that time, I promise we shall sail home."

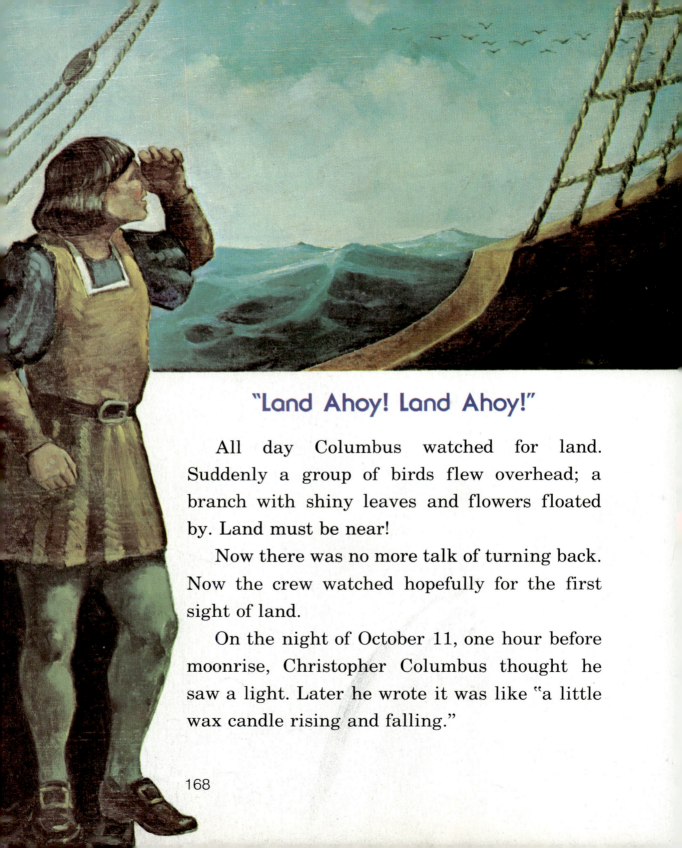

"Land Ahoy! Land Ahoy!"

All day Columbus watched for land. Suddenly a group of birds flew overhead; a branch with shiny leaves and flowers floated by. Land must be near!

Now there was no more talk of turning back. Now the crew watched hopefully for the first sight of land.

On the night of October 11, one hour before moonrise, Christopher Columbus thought he saw a light. Later he wrote it was like "a little wax candle rising and falling."

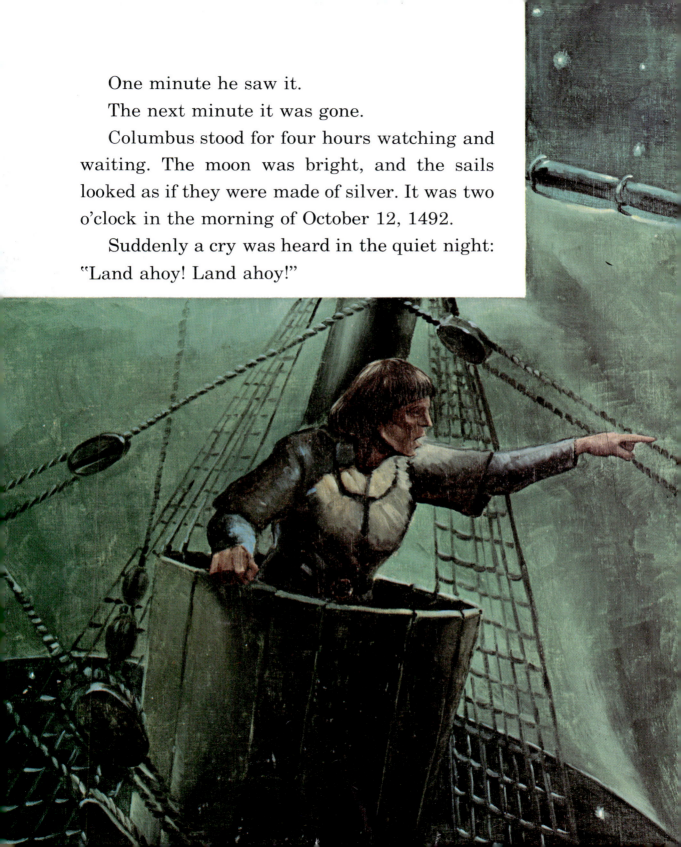

One minute he saw it.

The next minute it was gone.

Columbus stood for four hours watching and waiting. The moon was bright, and the sails looked as if they were made of silver. It was two o'clock in the morning of October 12, 1492.

Suddenly a cry was heard in the quiet night: "Land ahoy! Land ahoy!"

Christopher Columbus looked. He saw a sandy beach shining in the moonlight, and behind the beach, a forest of tall trees.

It had taken sixty-nine days, but the voyage was over.

Quickly Columbus dressed in his best clothes. As soon as it was light enough, the crew lowered the boats.

A few minutes later Columbus stood on the soil of a new land. He got down on his knees to kiss the ground.

As he rejoiced, tears of joy streamed down his face, for he knew that he had succeeded. He rose, planted the flag of Spain in the new land, and called the island San Salvador.

(To be read by the teacher.)

Dream Song

At night may I roam,
Against the winds may I roam,
At night may I roam,
When the owl is hooting may I roam.

At dawn may I roam,
Against the winds may I roam,
At dawn may I roam,
When the crow is calling may I roam.

SIOUXIAN MEDICINE SONG

Amelia Earhart,
First Lady of Flight

Adapted by SUSAN SMITH

As a small girl Amelia Earhart enjoyed doing exciting things. She grew up and became the first woman to cross the Atlantic Ocean by plane, the first woman to fly across the Atlantic alone. How did Amelia Earhart fall in love with flying? It may have started the day she turned nine years old.

It was July 24, 1907, Amelia's ninth birthday, and Papa had promised to take his daughter to the State Fair. Amelia had never been to a big fair before, and this one was everything she'd hoped for—and more. She loved the colors, sounds, crowds, and excitement. Where to go first? What to do?

Suddenly a loud voice shouted, "In one half hour the big event of the Fair—the flying airplane—will take off from South Field. Hurry! Don't miss it."

"*That's* something we surely don't want to miss!" Mr. Earhart said as he took Amelia's hand

and walked swiftly to the South Field where a crowd had already collected.

"Papa, I can't see a thing!" said Amelia. Her father pointed to the sky and said, "Can you see up there, Amelia?"

"Yes, of course, Papa."

"Well, all you need to do is watch the sky."

"What *is* an airplane, Papa?" asked Amelia.

"It's a machine that flies in the air," he said. "A person drives it; it's kind of like a car that goes in the air."

"Papa," Amelia said, "lift me up so I can see the airplane right now!" Mr. Earhart lifted his tall daughter up so that she could see.

"You don't mean he's going up into the sky in *that*!" Amelia shouted in amazement. "He'll be sure to get killed."

The flying machine was made mostly of wood. There were two broad thin boards, one above the other; a man sat between those two winglike boards, his feet resting on a steering bar. Behind the man was a big motor. The tail of the airplane looked like a box kite. And the whole thing rested on three wheels, two in front, one in back.

"Papa," Amelia cried, "it's starting!" A man turned a flat wooden board that was hooked to the motor. Then the board began to whirl faster and faster, and the machine, pushed by two people, started moving slowly down the field.

The noises from the motor grew louder and louder. The thing was moving more quickly along the grass. Then it was speeding. "Look," Amelia

screamed out, "it's going up into the *air*!" But her words were lost in the cheers of the crowd.

Amelia got down and stood on the ground. She could see very well from there now, for the strange machine was in the *sky*. It was flying right above them. Amelia stared in silence, her eyes and her mouth wide open as the airplane swooped around in the sky like a giant, noisy bird.

"Papa!" Amelia shouted, "it's the most exciting thing I've ever seen in my whole life!"

Though she still didn't understand why and how a plane flew, there was one thing she did know. She wanted to fly!

Many years went by. But Amelia never forgot her dream of learning to fly. She grew older and got out of school. One day Amelia went to another air show. As she watched the planes she asked her father, "How much does it cost to learn how to fly?"

"I'd say about a thousand dollars," he said.

"Well," said Amelia, "I'm going to fly tomorrow! I can't pay for lessons, but I can pay for a ride, anyway." She ran over to a person who worked at the air show and asked him to book her for a flight the next day.

The next morning as Amelia and her father walked across the field, Amelia kept looking up into the sunny blue sky. It seemed hard to believe—in a short while she would be *up* there!

A man in a pilot's suit came up to them and said to Mr. Earhart, "All set to go up, sir?"

"Not *me*!" said Mr. Earhart. "It's my daughter Amelia who wants to fly."

The pilot looked surprised. Then he smiled and said, "I'm your pilot." Amelia shook hands and said, "I'm Amelia Earhart."

The pilot helped her climb into the plane and then climbed in after her. "Contact!" he shouted, and a man turned the propeller until, with a great roar, the plane moved down the runway. Suddenly the plane rose into the air. It flew high into the morning sky.

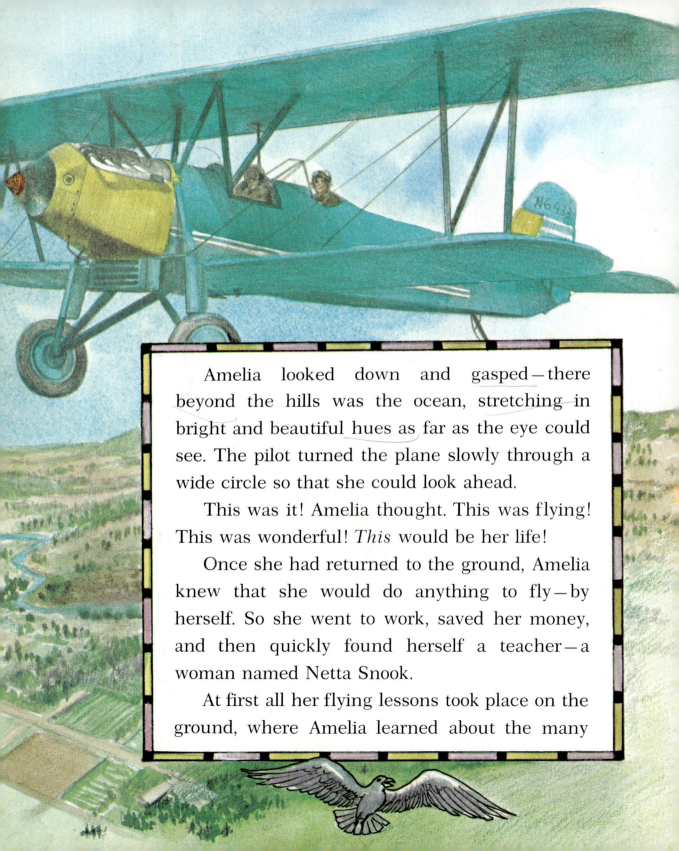

Amelia looked down and gasped—there beyond the hills was the ocean, stretching in bright and beautiful hues as far as the eye could see. The pilot turned the plane slowly through a wide circle so that she could look ahead.

This was it! Amelia thought. This was flying! This was wonderful! *This* would be her life!

Once she had returned to the ground, Amelia knew that she would do anything to fly—by herself. So she went to work, saved her money, and then quickly found herself a teacher—a woman named Netta Snook.

At first all her flying lessons took place on the ground, where Amelia learned about the many different parts of a plane, what each part did, and how to fix it if it broke. Amelia learned swiftly.

Soon she and Netta were ready to fly in the air together. The plane had two sets of controls so that Netta could fix mistakes that Amelia made. Again Amelia learned quickly.

Finally the day came when Amelia was ready to fly by herself. Amelia climbed slowly into her plane and sat, for the first time, alone. She wondered, would she remember everything? How could she possibly remember all the things she had learned?

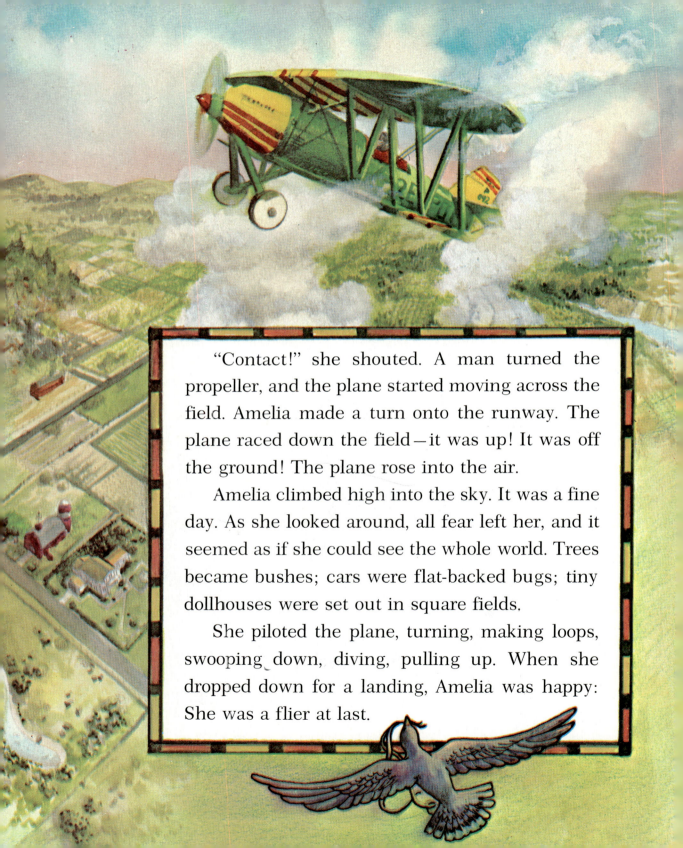

"Contact!" she shouted. A man turned the propeller, and the plane started moving across the field. Amelia made a turn onto the runway. The plane raced down the field—it was up! It was off the ground! The plane rose into the air.

Amelia climbed high into the sky. It was a fine day. As she looked around, all fear left her, and it seemed as if she could see the whole world. Trees became bushes; cars were flat-backed bugs; tiny dollhouses were set out in square fields.

She piloted the plane, turning, making loops, swooping down, diving, pulling up. When she dropped down for a landing, Amelia was happy: She was a flier at last.

She landed with a huge bump, rolled along the runway, and came to a stop.

"How do you feel, Amelia?" one of the pilots shouted to her.

"Happy," Amelia said, speaking more to herself than to him, "happier than I've ever been in my life."

(To be read by the teacher.)

A Song of Greatness

When I hear the old men
Telling of heroes,
Telling of great deeds
Of ancient days,
When I hear that telling
Then I think within me
I too am one of these.

When I hear the people
Praising great ones,
Then I know that I too
Shall be esteemed,
I too when my time comes
Shall do mightily.

MARY AUSTIN

A Brave Explorer
by LANGSTON HUGHES

A man in worn knee pants and a hat stood on a high mesa in the fierce sun. He looked across a golden desert. Beyond the desert, as far as one could see, were only mountains.

The man was Estevan, called by his friends Estevanico. He was looking for the Seven Cities of Cibola that he had heard were built of gold. The Indians who showed him the way into the Southwest knew nothing about such cities. They simply wondered what this strange person was looking for and why he had come into this desert country.

Estevanico, whose Spanish name meant Kid Steve, was born in Africa. He became an explorer, fearless and full of the love of adventure.

He sailed from Spain with a group of five hundred men looking for new lands beyond the seas. They landed on the coast of Florida. But the Spaniards underwent terrible times—in less than three months, a strange sickness killed half of them.

The men set sail again. This time their ship was wrecked. All the people were killed in the shipwreck except Estevanico and three others.

For more than eight years, these four men wandered across the country, living with kindly Indians. Estevanico learned to speak many Indian languages, which helped him in his travels. He wandered as far south as Mexico City where he stayed for a while.

But Estevanico did not like to stay in one place long, so in 1539 he joined a group looking for the fabulous Seven Cities of Cibola. The group set out to the north over the mountains and across the plains.

Now Estevanico looked over the desert land, wondering about the cities of gold. The summer was very hot. Before it was over, the others were too tired to go on. They asked Estevanico if he would go ahead with a group of Indian runners. If he found rich lands or golden cities, they told him to send someone back with word and they would join him.

The Indian runners could not speak Spanish, and the Spaniards did not know the Indians' language. So Estevanico worked out a plan for sending back messages. He would send back a cross every few days. Its size would show how far he had gone and how important his discoveries were.

A little wooden cross the size of a hand, made from twigs, would mean that he had found nothing special. But if he found cities of gold or fabulous riches, he would cut branches from a larger tree and send back a bigger cross.

At first the Indian runners brought back only very small crosses made of twigs. Estevanico was traveling across a rough and dangerous land where nobody lived. Heat, sand flies, mountain lions, cold nights, and blazing hot days forced him to go slowly. Dangerous animals ran through the rocky passes. There were a great many snakes. Sometimes a blue racer rushed across the path, or Estevanico met a rattler in an angry coil.

But Estevanico kept on going across the sands, beyond the mountains. He kept looking for the gold and riches of the fabulous land he hoped was just ahead. Meanwhile the others waited for news from him.

One day two Indians, tired and worn out from the heat, came into the camp. They carried a cross as tall as a person. Then the Spaniards knew that Estevanico had found a wonderful land somewhere in the desert. Perhaps he had even found the Seven Cities of Cibola! Quickly the Spaniards broke camp. They followed the Indian runners toward the new country which the explorer, Estevanico, had discovered.

The Spaniards soon found out why Estevanico had sent back the huge cross. He had not found any golden cities, but he had discovered the great pueblos built by the Zuñi Indians. The brave explorer, Estevanico, had found fabulous cities in what are today the states of Arizona and New Mexico.

Skills Lesson: Topical Organization

Helpful Headings

Suppose you had a book about countries of the world, and you were reading about Mexico. How would you quickly find information about the topic of Mexican art?

1. Open the book and read until you found the information you wanted.

2. Look here and there until you found something about Mexican art.

3. Read the topic headings to find the section that has the information.

Topic headings in books make information easy to find. Have you ever read a book that had topic headings?

The book below shows topic headings about our language. The English language has been changing and growing for a long time. Many of the words in our language have very interesting histories.

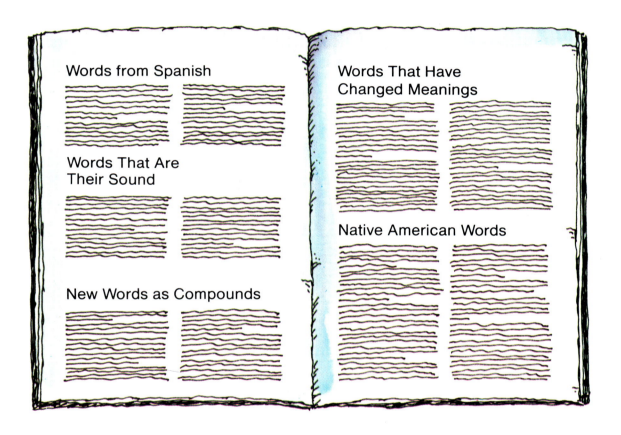

Read the headings. Then read the words and the information given about each word on the next page. Under which topic heading would you find each word?

pueblo: This word comes from the Spanish word for village.

meat: This word was once used for food of any kind, but is now used only for animal's flesh.

canoe: This word, first used by Native Americans, means a long, narrow boat.

purr: This is the sound of a happy cat.

boardwalk: This word means a walk made of boards, often beside a beach.

nice: Five hundred years ago, this word meant foolish!

You read about three explorers in this unit. List each one under the correct topic headings below. Some can be listed under more than one heading. Write or tell your answers.

Early Explorers of America   Sailors
Explorers from Spain   Fliers

World of Mystery

The Case of the Rubber Pillow

by DONALD J. SOBOL

During the summer Encyclopedia Brown worked as a detective for children who lived in the neighborhood. Every morning he put out this sign:

Late one morning Danny, a neighbor, ran into Detective Brown's office and put down some money on the table beside Encyclopedia.

"I want you to find my missing pillow," said Danny.

"I've seen a candy box and a boardwalk, but I've never worked on a pillowcase," said Encyclopedia thoughtfully.

"My pillow doesn't have a case," said Danny. "It's made of rubber—I blow it up on camping trips."

"Hmm," said Encyclopedia, "and it gave you the air. When?"

"Half an hour ago," said Danny. "I think Bugs Meany took it."

"Bugs?" said Encyclopedia, his voice becoming serious. Bugs Meany was known to be a troublemaker.

"I'll take the case," said Encyclopedia, "but please, let's have the whole story."

"Early this morning," said Danny, "Mom and I were painting the wood on the front of our house—the three front steps, the porch railing and posts, and the front door. We painted everything white."

"Where was the rubber pillow?" asked Encyclopedia.

"It was hanging on the clothesline at the side of the house," said Danny. "After we finished painting, Mom went in the back to clean up. I saw Bugs running away from the clothesline; he was carrying the pillow."

"Did your mother see him, too?"

"No, bad luck," said Danny. "It will be my word against Bugs's."

Encyclopedia closed his eyes and for a few minutes he did some deep thinking. Then he said, "We've got to trap Bugs—we've got to catch him in a lie!"

"It won't be easy," said Danny. "He's a very smart fellow."

The two boys rode their bicycles to Bugs's hangout, an unused tool house behind Ms. Hunt's Fix-it Shop.

Bugs was there alone, playing with some cards. "Get lost," he said.

"I will when you return Danny's pillow," said Encyclopedia.

"You took my rubber pillow from the clothesline at my house half an hour ago," said Danny angrily.

"Rubber pillow? Man, has this fellow's mouth heard from his brain lately?" barked Bugs. "I've never been near his house in my whole life."

"Why don't you tell that to Danny's mother?" said Encyclopedia. "She was behind the house, so she must have seen you taking the pillow."

Bugs nearly choked on the grass he was chewing, but he recovered himself and said, "I've been right here all morning."

"Then you wouldn't mind going with us to Danny's house," said Encyclopedia. "You're going to have to speak with his mother sooner or later."

"W-well, ahh, O.K.," muttered Bugs. "But you lead the way. Remember, I don't even know where he lives."

Outside Danny whispered, "My mother and father went off fishing, so there's nobody at home now."

"Don't worry," said Encyclopedia, "Bugs is far too sure of himself. He'll make a mistake."

The three boys rode over to Danny's house,

which was green with a white wood porch, door, and front steps.

"Go up and ring the doorbell," Encyclopedia dared Bugs.

Bugs kicked down the stand of his bicycle and looked at Danny's house. He looked at Danny. He seemed to be getting up his nerve. Suddenly he made up his mind.

"Watch me," he said.

He ran across the front yard and jumped over the three white wooden steps. His heel hit the floor of the porch and he tripped, but he righted himself without having to hold on to the railing. He looked back at Danny and Encyclopedia and grinned proudly.

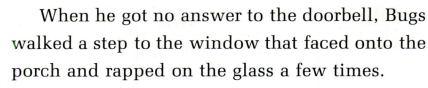

When he got no answer to the doorbell, Bugs walked a step to the window that faced onto the porch and rapped on the glass a few times.

"There's nobody home," he yelled to Encyclopedia. He left the porch, again leaping over the three steps.

"Your plan to trap him didn't work," said Danny sadly.

"Oh, yes it did!" said Encyclopedia.

He went to Bugs and spoke into the bigger boy's left ear.

As Bugs listened his fists tightened; angry stars seemed to shoot from his ears, and low, fighting sounds rolled in his throat.

But he said, "Awh...."

He got on his bike, a beaten fellow. Five minutes later he rode back up with Danny's rubber pillow.

"What did you say to him?" asked Danny after Bugs had gone off.

"Not very much; I just pointed out his mistake," said the boy detective. "In this case, what he did spoke louder than what he said."

WHAT WAS BUGS'S MISTAKE?

Answer to the Case of the Rubber Pillow

Bugs said he had never been to Danny's house, yet he didn't touch the porch railing, the steps, or the front door. He knew they had just been painted and were still wet.

Sound Effects for a Radio Play

by DINA ANASTASIO

Have you ever listened to a radio play? Did you wonder how the sound effects were made? Several, such as blood-chilling screams and moans, are not hard to work out. They are made by people doing the play. Others, such as thunder and rain, are harder to do.

Thunder. The sound of thunder is made with a large piece of sheet metal. If you shake it softly, the thunder rumbles. If you give it a hard, sudden shake, the metal sounds remarkably like the loud crack of thunder.

When doing a radio play at home or in your schoolroom, you can use a large metal cookie sheet or pan. But a piece of sheet metal will sound more like thunder.

Footsteps. Footsteps can be fun to make. Place a pair of shoes on your hands and "walk" or "run" the shoes to make the sound of footsteps.

If the people in the play are walking across the floor, just walk the shoes, hard, across the floor. If the people are walking along a stone path, fill a box loosely with small stones and walk the shoes on the stones.

Most fun of all are the sounds of shoes on creaky floors or stairs. Find a long board and put a brick under each end. Walk your shoes in the middle of the board. The board will bend and creak, just as if one were walking along an old floor.

Rain. You can make the sound of rain by pouring water from a watering can onto a metal sheet. The harder the water pours, the louder the sound of falling rain will become.

Another way to make the sound is to turn an FM radio to an empty station. The hiss of the empty station sounds surprisingly like the sound of steadily falling rain. If the rain is not falling hard enough, turn up the sound of the radio so that the hiss is louder.

Wind. The sound of wind is lots of fun to make and can be made in many ways. A number of people can work together to make it by softly going "whoo-o-o-o, whoo-o-o-o." Whistling wind sounds can also be made by gently blowing across the top of a soda bottle.

Squeaking door. If you have a door that squeaks, you are lucky, for many radio plays call for "squeaking doors." If not, you can make this noise by running a nail across a piece of glass or a pan. A swivel chair often sounds like a squeaking door when it moves, and is sometimes used to make these sounds.

Telephone. Telephones on radio shows really ring, but you can make the sound in your classroom with a bell. The person "at the other end of the line" speaks through a piece of cloth so that the voice sounds far away.

These are some of the ways you can make sound effects for a radio play. When you put on the play that follows, why don't you try some of them out?

The Haunted House
A Radio Play

by DINA ANASTASIO

(Sounds: eerie music; eerie whistling)

NARRATOR: It was a huge old house on a lonely country road, and many people said it was haunted. No one had been near the house in years until one stormy summer day . . .

(Sounds: rain; thunder; gusts of wind)

NARRATOR: Sandy, Linda, David, and John visited it, and Sandy decided that there was no such thing as a ghost.

SANDY: You three are silly. What if the house is old? There are no *ghosts* in it.

LINDA: I'm not so sure of that, Sandy.

SANDY: I'll prove it to you, Linda. David, John, and Linda, meet me here at seven o'clock. We'll go inside and hunt for ghosts.

DAVID: I'm not going to come.

SANDY: Why not, David?

DAVID: I *know* this house is full of ghosts! John, *you* go with Sandy.

JOHN: Not on your life! I'm staying right where I belong tonight—at home in bed!

LINDA: You won't get me near that eerie place!

SANDY: Talk about silly! There's no such thing as a haunted house and I'll prove it. Come on, now, David, are you going to be a scaredy cat?

DAVID: O.K., I'll come . . . I'm not scared.

SANDY: All right then, at seven o'clock in front of this house, David.

DAVID: I sure hope this storm lets up.

(Sounds: crash of thunder; then, music)

NARRATOR: At six o'clock that evening, John called Linda on the phone.

(Sound: telephone rings)

LINDA: Hello.

JOHN: Hi, Linda, this is John. Listen, are you really afraid to go up to that house?

LINDA: Yes, I really am.

JOHN: Well, so am I, but I've got an idea that might make it worth going there anyway.

LINDA: What is it?

JOHN: Let's go there right now and hide. When Sandy and David come in, we'll make noises and crashes and things like that.

LINDA: You mean we'll scare them!

JOHN: That's the idea, Linda!

LINDA: I'll meet you there.

NARRATOR: Of course, Sandy and David knew nothing about John and Linda's plan. At seven o'clock Sandy and David walked slowly up to the old house.

(Sounds: wind; thunder; rain)

DAVID: Wow, this place is eerie!

SANDY: Come on, let's go inside.

(Sound: footsteps on creaking steps)

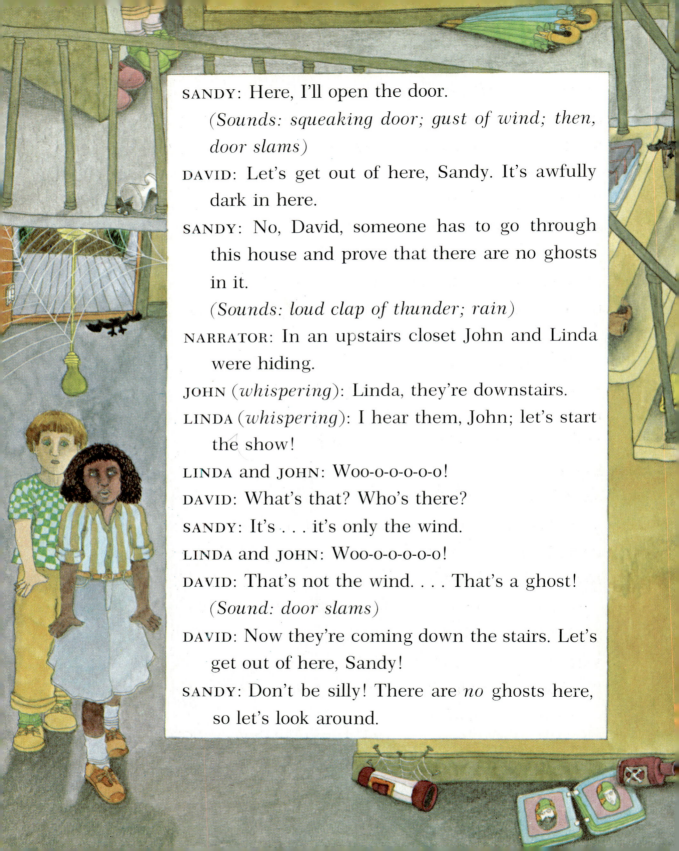

SANDY: Here, I'll open the door.
 (*Sounds: squeaking door; gust of wind; then, door slams*)
DAVID: Let's get out of here, Sandy. It's awfully dark in here.
SANDY: No, David, someone has to go through this house and prove that there are no ghosts in it.
 (*Sounds: loud clap of thunder; rain*)
NARRATOR: In an upstairs closet John and Linda were hiding.
JOHN (*whispering*): Linda, they're downstairs.
LINDA (*whispering*): I hear them, John; let's start the show!
LINDA and JOHN: Woo-o-o-o-o-o!
DAVID: What's that? Who's there?
SANDY: It's . . . it's only the wind.
LINDA and JOHN: Woo-o-o-o-o-o!
DAVID: That's not the wind. . . . That's a ghost!
 (*Sound: door slams*)
DAVID: Now they're coming down the stairs. Let's get out of here, Sandy!
SANDY: Don't be silly! There are *no* ghosts here, so let's look around.

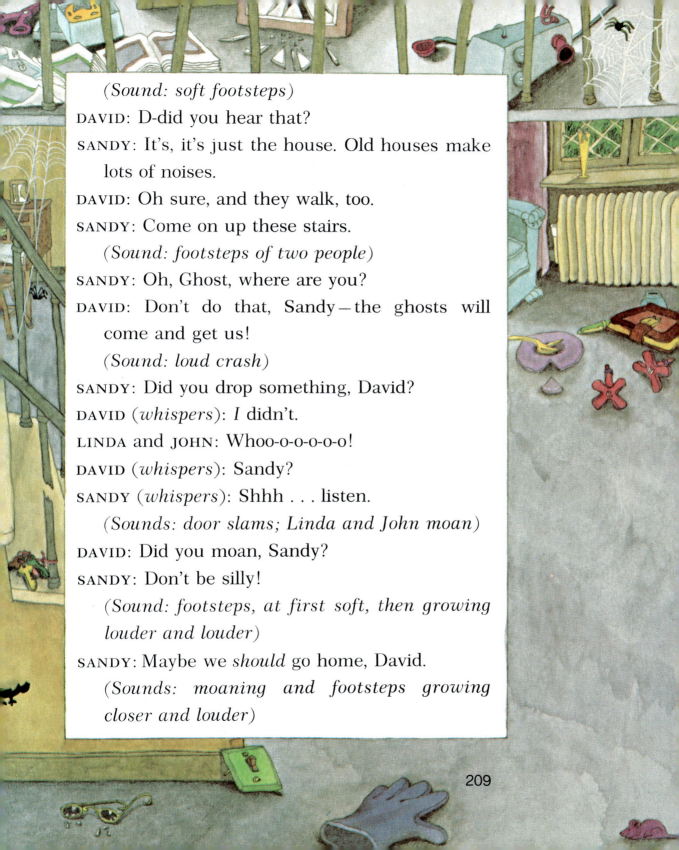

(*Sound: soft footsteps*)

DAVID: D-did you hear that?

SANDY: It's, it's just the house. Old houses make lots of noises.

DAVID: Oh sure, and they walk, too.

SANDY: Come on up these stairs.

(*Sound: footsteps of two people*)

SANDY: Oh, Ghost, where are you?

DAVID: Don't do that, Sandy—the ghosts will come and get us!

(*Sound: loud crash*)

SANDY: Did you drop something, David?

DAVID (*whispers*): *I* didn't.

LINDA and JOHN: Whoo-o-o-o-o-o!

DAVID (*whispers*): Sandy?

SANDY (*whispers*): Shhh . . . listen.

(*Sounds: door slams; Linda and John moan*)

DAVID: Did *you* moan, Sandy?

SANDY: Don't be silly!

(*Sound: footsteps, at first soft, then growing louder and louder*)

SANDY: Maybe we *should* go home, David.

(*Sounds: moaning and footsteps growing closer and louder*)

209

DAVID (*frightened whisper*): You bet! Let's get out of here!
(*Sounds: two pairs of footsteps racing down the stairs; door slams; two pairs of footsteps running down stony road*)
DAVID (*breathlessly*): Hee-elp!
NARRATOR: And that took care of the two ghost-hunters! But what about John and Linda?
JOHN (*laughing*): Did you see them, Linda?
LINDA (*laughing*): Wait till I ask Sandy if she saw any ghosts. What do you think she'll say?

JOHN: I can't imagine. Well, let's get out of here.
   (*Sound: footsteps on creaking stairs*)
JOHN: Watch out on these stairs, Linda, it's really dark in here.
LINDA: I wish we had a light.
JOHN: There's a light in that room down there, see it?
LINDA: John! There can't be a light there.
JOHN: There is.
LINDA: Oh, oh! We'd better get out of here!
   (*Sounds: running feet; door bangs shut; loud crash of thunder; then, eerie whistling*)
NARRATOR (*very slowly, in an eerie voice*): Without looking back, John and Linda ran down the dark country road. And behind them in the window of the house, a small light gleamed brightly in the darkness.
   (*Sound: eerie music*)

Nate the Great

by MARJORIE WEINMAN SHARMAT

I, Nate the Great, am a busy detective.

One morning I was not busy. I was on my vacation. I was sitting under a tree enjoying a peaceful day with my dog, Sludge, and a pancake. He needed a vacation, too.

My friend Claude came into the yard. I knew that he had lost something. Claude was always losing things.

"I lost my way to your house," he said, "and then I found it."

"What else did you lose?" I asked.

"I lost the list I was taking to the food store. Can you help me find it?"

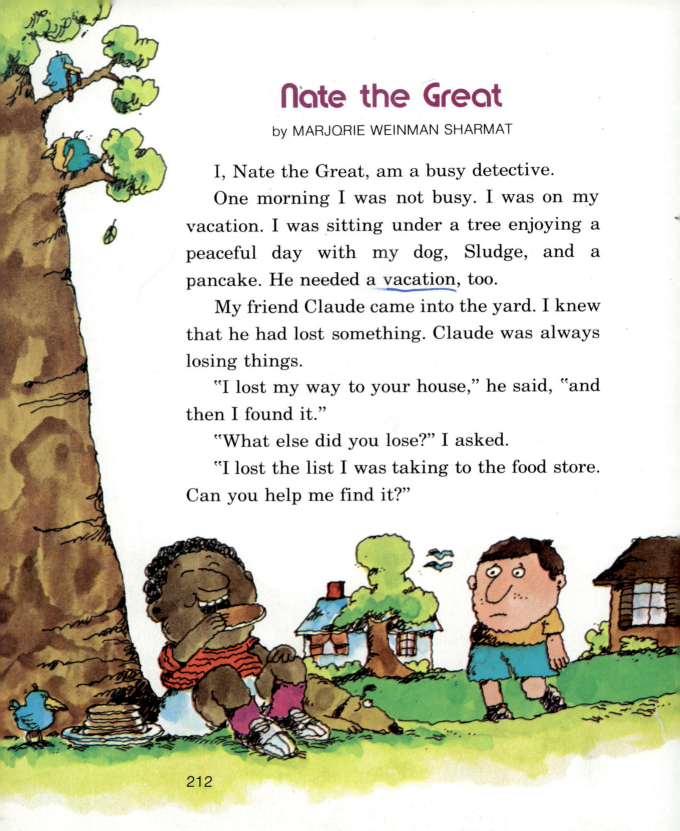

"Very well," I said. "I, Nate the Great, will take your case. Tell me, what was on the list?"

"If I could remember, I wouldn't need the list," Claude said.

"Can you remember some of the list?"

"Yes," Claude said, "I remember salt, milk, butter, flour, sugar, and tuna fish."

"What streets did you walk on?" I asked.

"I'm not sure," Claude said. "I lost my way a few times."

"Then I, Nate the Great, know what to do. I will draw a map of every street between your house and the food store and we will follow the map."

Sludge and I got up. Our vacation was over. I got a piece of paper and a pen. I drew a map on the piece of paper.

Claude said, "I will walk with you."

"Don't get lost," I said, "or I will have two cases to solve." We walked between Claude's house and the food store and then between the food store and Claude's house. Sludge sniffed. But we could not find the list.

"Perhaps it blew away," I said. I dropped the map to the ground.

"What are you doing?" Claude asked.

"I am dropping the map. Whichever direction it goes will show us the way the wind is blowing. Perhaps your list blew in the same direction."

The map blew along the pavement toward Rosamond's house and disappeared. "I will go to Rosamond's house," I said. "I will ask her if she has seen your list."

"I will go back to my house and wait," Claude said.

"We are in front of your house," I said.

"Yes, that makes it very easy to find," Claude said.

Sludge and I went to Rosamond's house. Rosamond opened the door. Rosamond is a very

strange girl. Today she looked more than strange. She looked strange and white. She was covered with flour. Sludge sniffed hard. I sniffed hard. Rosamond smelled delicious. Pancakes! She was making pancakes.

We walked in. Rosamond's four black cats were there. Today they were white, too. The cats looked at Sludge. They were not afraid of him. Nobody is afraid of Sludge.

"I am making cat-pancakes for my cats," Rosamond said, "from a new recipe."

"I am curious. I would like to taste cat-pancakes," I said.

"You are not a cat," Rosamond said.

"I would like to taste them anyway," I said. "A pancake is a pancake." Rosamond and I sat down. I ate a pancake. It tasted fishy. I ate another. It tasted fishier.

"I am looking for Claude's food list," I said. "I think the wind blew it toward your house. Have you seen it?"

"I haven't seen a list," Rosamond said. "But—I am having a cat-pancake party this morning, and I have invited all the cats I know. Can you come?"

"I am not a cat," I said.

"That's what I told you before," Rosamond said.

I thanked Rosamond for her pancakes. Then Sludge and I walked up the pavement to Claude's house. Claude was home. He was not lost. It was a good sign.

"I, Nate the Great, have not found your list,"

I said. "Can you remember anything else that was written on it?"

"I remember! I remember two more things," Claude said. "Eggs and baking powder."

"Very good," I said.

"Can you find the list before lunch?"

"I hope so," I said. "Come to my house at eleven."

Sludge and I walked home slowly. This was a hard case.

At home I made myself some pancakes. I mixed eggs, flour, salt, baking powder, milk, butter, and sugar together and cooked them.

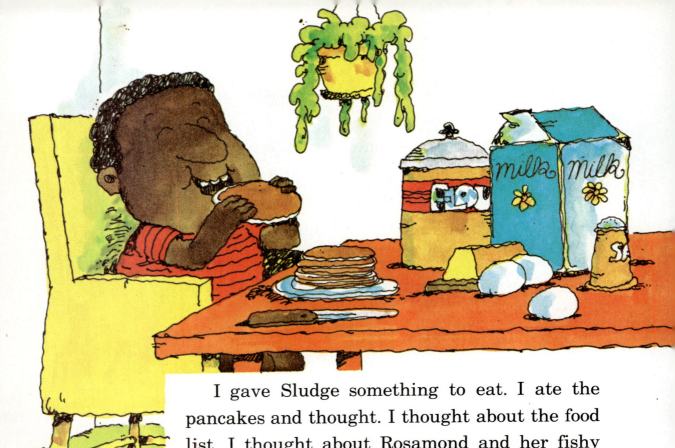

I gave Sludge something to eat. I ate the pancakes and thought. I thought about the food list. I thought about Rosamond and her fishy cat-pancakes. I put ideas together. I took them apart.

Then I had a big idea. I knew I must go back to Rosamond's house. I did not want to do that. I did not want to be at a party with Rosamond and all the cats she knew. But I had a job to do. I had a case to solve.

Sludge and I walked quickly to Rosamond's house. I said hello to Rosamond and more cats than I could count.

"I came to talk about your cat-pancakes," I said.

"Would you like more?" Rosamond asked.

"I would like to see your recipe," I said.

"Here it is," Rosamond said.

"This is curious. There are no directions in this recipe," I said.

"I don't need any," Rosamond said. "I just mix some of everything together."

"Tell me, where did you get this recipe?"

"I found it today," Rosamond said.

"Aha! You found it," I said. "Did you find it near your house?"

"Yes," Rosamond said. "How did you know that?"

"I have something to tell you. I, Nate the Great, say that your cat-pancake recipe is Claude's missing list." I stood tall. I cleared my throat. Forcefully I read the recipe: "Salt, milk, butter, flour, tuna fish, eggs, baking powder, sugar."

"Oh!" Rosamond said. "When I found the paper, I thought it was a cat-pancake recipe."

"Yes," I said. "When you saw the food list, you thought it was what you hoped it was. A cat-pancake recipe.

"I, Nate the Great, thought of that when I was making pancakes. I mixed eggs, flour, salt, baking powder, milk, butter, and sugar. Claude had told me they were on his list. The other thing he remembered on the list was tuna fish. Cats like tuna fish. So — cat-pancakes!"

"Oh," Rosamond said, "well, Claude can have his paper back. I will keep the recipe in my head."

"That is a good place for it," I said. "It cannot blow away."

I said good-by to Rosamond and more cats than I could count. Sludge and I went home with the list. The case was solved. And it was almost eleven o'clock.

When Claude comes at eleven, I will give him his list.

It is now past eleven o'clock. It is now past eleven-thirty. Claude has not shown up and I do not see him anywhere. I hope Claude has not lost himself.

It is now past twelve. Here comes Claude. I am glad I do not have to look for him. I am glad the case is over. I, Nate the Great, have something important to do.

I, Nate the Great, am going to finish my vacation.

Skills Lesson: Fact and Opinion

Fact or Opinion?

Facts are true information about something. Opinions are what someone thinks about something. Read the following sentences and tell whether each is a fact or an opinion.

Rover is a small dog with long ears.
Rover is a wonderful dog.

If you said that the first sentence tells facts and the second tells an opinion, you are right. The first sentence gives you information about Rover. The second tells you what the writer thinks about Rover.

TRY THIS

What is your favorite food? Write or tell some facts and opinions about it. Have a friend try to tell which sentences are facts and which are your opinions. Does your friend agree with your opinions?

Facts and Opinions in Stories

In this mystery story, the facts give us information. The characters' opinions tell us what they think about something. Look for the facts and opinions as you read.

As Peter was getting ready for school, he saw that one of his shoes was missing. "I put both shoes under the bed last night," thought Peter. "Now I have only one shoe. I bet Sandy took my shoe. She always plays jokes on me."

Peter ran down to the kitchen.

"Sandy," he said, "you took my shoe!"

"Where did you get your facts?" asked Sandy. "I didn't take your shoe. I think you forgot where you put it. Remember, I went to sleep before you, and I got up after you did."

"I remember putting both shoes under my bed last night," said Peter. "Then Rover came in to play. Where could my shoe be?"

What do you think happened to Peter's shoe? What facts helped you to figure it out? What facts and opinions did Peter give? What facts and opinions did Sandy give? Why do you think the author mixed facts and opinions?

TRY THIS

Below are some sentences about the stories in this unit. Tell whether each statement is a fact or an opinion.

1. All the stories are mysteries.
2. The best story is "The Haunted House."
3. "The Case of the Rubber Pillow" is very funny.
4. Nate's dog is named Sludge.

Today and Tomorrow

TOMORROW'S WORLD

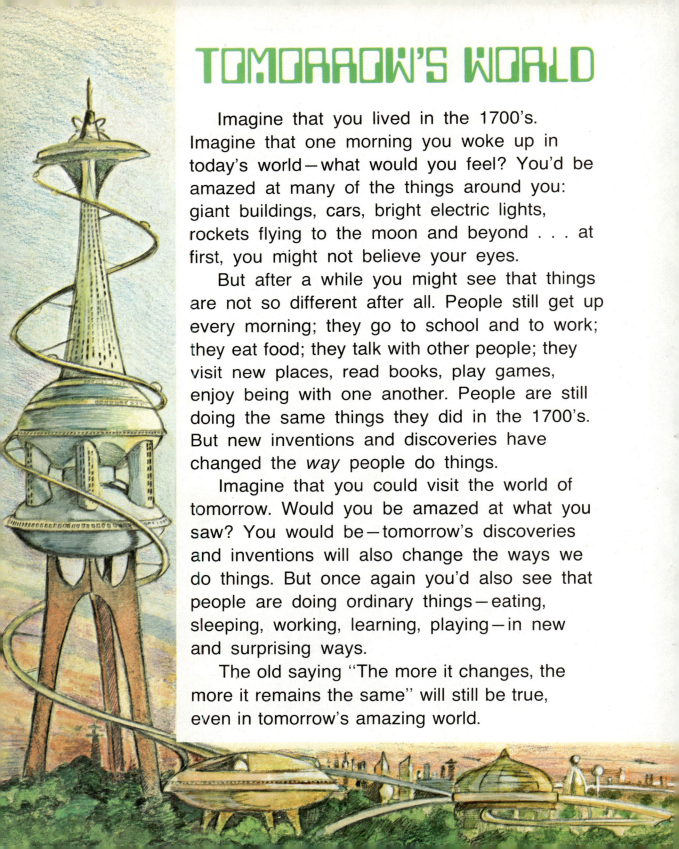

Imagine that you lived in the 1700's. Imagine that one morning you woke up in today's world—what would you feel? You'd be amazed at many of the things around you: giant buildings, cars, bright electric lights, rockets flying to the moon and beyond . . . at first, you might not believe your eyes.

But after a while you might see that things are not so different after all. People still get up every morning; they go to school and to work; they eat food; they talk with other people; they visit new places, read books, play games, enjoy being with one another. People are still doing the same things they did in the 1700's. But new inventions and discoveries have changed the *way* people do things.

Imagine that you could visit the world of tomorrow. Would you be amazed at what you saw? You would be—tomorrow's discoveries and inventions will also change the ways we do things. But once again you'd also see that people are doing ordinary things—eating, sleeping, working, learning, playing—in new and surprising ways.

The old saying "The more it changes, the more it remains the same" will still be true, even in tomorrow's amazing world.

TOMORROW: *Exploring the Sea*

People have always been curious to discover more about the earth. For thousands of years we knew very little; maps of the world had large empty spaces where map makers sometimes wrote: "Here there be dragons." No one had ever visited those places, so who could tell? Perhaps there *were* dragons in those unknown places.

As time passed, people went to those unknown lands and explored them. They found valleys and mountains, plains and forests, but not once did they find any dragons. The map makers happily fixed their maps.

Today most of the lands of the earth have been explored and mapped. We even have very good maps of places where no one has been, for we can take pictures of any part of the earth from outer space. It might seem, then, that we have very complete knowledge of our earth's surface.

But that isn't so. Two-thirds of our world is almost completely unfamiliar to us. That is the two-thirds of the world covered by ocean.

We have a rough idea of what the land under the ocean looks like. Look at this map; it shows how the earth would appear if the oceans were suddenly removed.

The land under the ocean is much like the land of the surface. There are mountains, plains, and valleys. But the mountains are taller, the plains larger, and the valleys deeper than those we know. And deep cracks, thousands of kilometers long, run down the

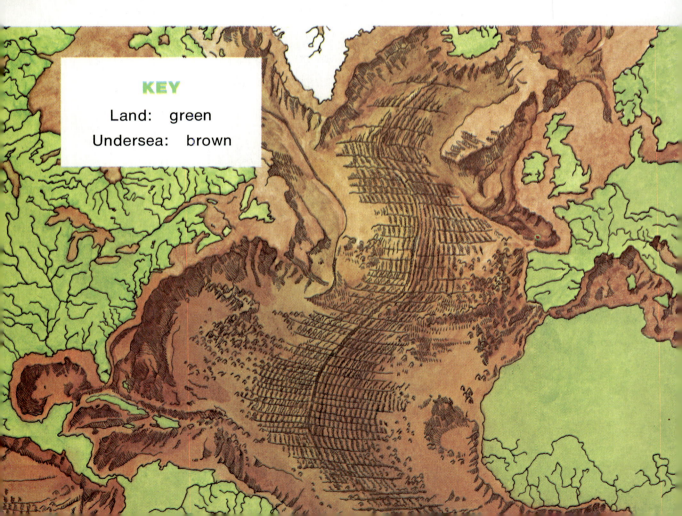

KEY
Land: green
Undersea: brown

middle of many ocean beds.

How much of the land under the ocean has been visited by explorers? Very little. It is not easy to explore the bottom of the ocean; the pressure of the deep water is so great that it will crush all but the hardest metals.

But we have built some very strong craft that can descend into parts of the ocean. Today we are beginning to explore the unknown two-thirds of our world. In some ways it may be as important to explore the sea as to explore outer space. In the ocean we may find many new and important things.

Underwater Craft

The deeper people descend into the ocean, the greater the pressure on their craft. So, very deep ocean exploration—below a kilometer or more—calls for a very strong craft indeed.

One kind of craft is a big ball with thick walls made of strong metal. It has thick, strong windows for underwater pictures. This craft can descend many kilometers into the water. It has returned with pictures of many strange fish that live there.

In the world of tomorrow, people will use other craft to explore the deep, dark parts of the ocean. *Deep Diver* can carry four people down to the bottom. It can stay down for some time. Divers can go in and out of the craft as they work on the ocean floor.

Submarines run by computers can also be used to explore deeper parts of the ocean. Small submarines and machines with metal arms will move about, dig, and do many kinds of work deep down in the sea.

A submarine with a metal arm works under the sea.

FLIP gets ready to flip over in the water.

When we explore shallow parts of the ocean near the land, we can use craft that are larger and less strong. One of the most curious of these is a funny-looking craft called FLIP. On top of the water it looks like a boat that is long and very thin at one end. The thin end can be filled with water. When the water is in, FLIP flips! The thin end sinks, and the ship stands straight up in the water; the other end, as high as a four-story building, sticks up in the air. Sea explorers live in this part, but go down into their underwater house to explore the ocean.

Sometimes FLIP floats this way for ten days at a time while the people on it explore the sea.

Many undersea explorers use diving gear when they explore the ocean. They carry a bottle of air on their backs, and wear fins so that they can swim like a fish. They are able to stay underwater for hours at a time. But of course they must come up out of the water before the air runs out.

Some divers work in the sea for days at a time without coming up to the surface. They live in an undersea building called a habitat, a hundred meters under the water. Teams of divers eat, sleep, and work in the habitat. They go out of a hatch, explore and work, and return to the habitat when their jobs are done.

Living Under the Sea

Many people believe that more and more habitats will be built undersea in times to come. More and more people will live their lives under the ocean. To them the sea will not be unknown and dangerous, but a friendly place where they will work and play.

One day there may be whole cities of habitats, filled with busy people, coming and going, making their livings from the sea. Here are some of the things that people of the future may do undersea.

Farming the Sea. Today people "hunt" for fish in much the way we used to hunt for animals long ago. They travel across the ocean searching for schools of fish. If they are lucky, they do find fish, and lift some of them up in nets.

Long ago people learned an easier way to get food—they learned to tame and herd animals. Wouldn't it be nice to do the same thing with fish?

Imagine the underwater farm of the future.

There is the farmer, in diving gear, watching over the schools of fish. And there is the farmer's dog, a dolphin, making sure that the fish do not misbehave by wandering off. The underwater farmer feeds the fish, and guards them, and uses them for food, just as today's land farmers do with their cattle.

Other farmers will grow and pick undersea plants, just as we grow and pick wheat and other land plants today.

Mining the Ocean. The ocean floor has many metals and other things we need. Someday people will drive machines across the floor of the ocean to the mine and dig up metals, just as we do on the land today.

They will also explore for oil, buried deep under the sea floor.

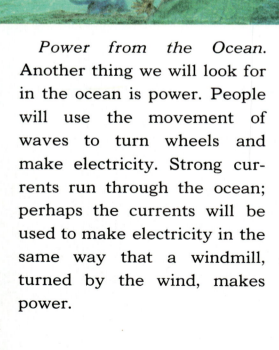

Power from the Ocean. Another thing we will look for in the ocean is power. People will use the movement of waves to turn wheels and make electricity. Strong currents run through the ocean; perhaps the currents will be used to make electricity in the same way that a windmill, turned by the wind, makes power.

People will find many other ways to use the ocean, and so more people will move into the sea. Slowly the shallow parts of the ocean will become crowded with habitats, farms, and workplaces until undersea cities encircle the land.

People will move into the deeper parts of the ocean. What will they find there? Will they find dragons? This is unlikely. Most likely they will find mountains and valleys, and new places to live.

What will it be like to live under the water? Will children play underwater tag? Will people go to underwater ballgames? Will families jump into their submarines and go for a picnic in some quiet undersea forest? Will children have dolphins as pets?

We do not really know yet. But all of these things, and many other unimaginable things, will take place when people of tomorrow begin to live under the sea.

TOMORROW: Moving Around

Perhaps one day people will move into the sea, but many people will still live on the land. How will those people travel about? How will tomorrow's children get to school?

Imagine this: You live in a large city fifty years in the future. One morning you wake up, get dressed for school, eat, and go downstairs to wait for the bus.

The street is crowded with trucks and jammed with cars—it is so crowded that not

238

one thing is moving. You wait for the bus; you wait all day and the bus never comes, because the traffic never moves! The city has become so crowded with cars and trucks that they can no longer move. All the space is used up!

Will this happen one day? Probably not—though it could happen if we do not plan ahead. Today's cities are growing very fast; they have more people, more cars and trucks each year. It could all end up in a huge traffic jam.

Imagine a different future fifty years from now. You wake up and go downstairs to wait for the bus. The street has cars and trucks on it, but it is not jammed; there are no cars parked by the sidewalk. The cars in the street are small and move quietly past you. Trucks go by, too, but no one is driving them! This is the kind of future we are hoping to have.

People are aware that today too much city space is taken up by freeways, streets, and parking lots. People who are making plans for tomorrow's cities hope to put much of the traffic underground.

Some planners also hope that all cars, trucks, and buses will be electric. Electric cars will not make the air dirty. And they will make very little noise as they move along.

Some people think that each electric car will have a small computer in its trunk. Cars controlled by computers will last longer and need fewer repairs. Computers will also drive the cars! The driver will push a few buttons and the computer will do the rest.

Highways, too, may have computers. Each highway will have electric wires built into the roadbed so that computers may control all the traffic that moves on the road.

Imagine what it may be like then to ride in your bus across the city. It will move by itself along the road under the control of a computer. No one will have to drive. The bus driver pushes a button to tell the computer where the bus has to go, and then everyone sits back and reads or looks out at traffic that is also moving along under computer control.

On a computer highway four times as much traffic will travel with far less danger than on a road of today.

NEW KINDS OF TRAINS

On longer trips people may be traveling in new ways. Some of these new ways of traveling on land will not need wheels, for air will take the place of wheels. New kinds of trains will move just above the ground, held up by a cushion of air.

The picture shows an air train in Japan. It glides just above its rail, which looks like a low wall. The air train speeds along on a very thin cushion of air. The air is pushed down by fans, and the train is pulled ahead by a giant propeller.

Tube trains are now being planned, too. Air from the front of the train will be pushed around the sides of the train to the back. Jets of air will shoot out the back as the train rockets ahead. Riding on a cushion of air, it may be able to move at a speed of almost one thousand kilometers an hour!

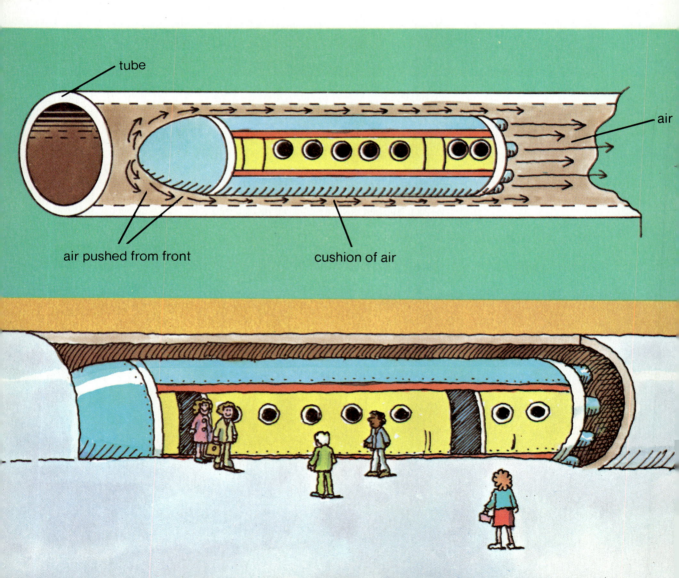

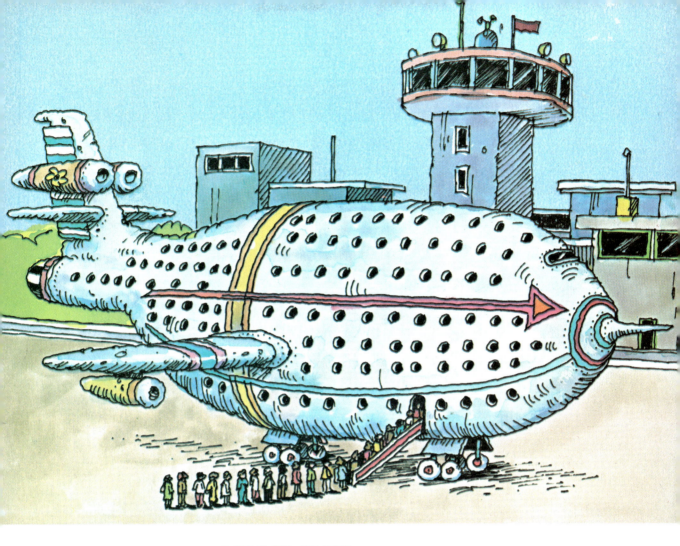

NEW PLANES

Before long there may be new planes bigger than any we now have. Compared to today's planes, these jets will be giants. Jets that seat one thousand people may someday be speeding silently across the sky.

Some of the jets will be rockets, and they will not be going to any spot on the earth. They'll be heading for stations in outer space.

Back on the earth helicopters and other smaller planes will be used for short trips. One new kind of smaller plane that has already been built doesn't need a long runway for take-off because it goes straight up from the ground into the air. This plane can do many of the things helicopters do. It can take off and land in a small space. And it can hover—stay in one place in the air—just as helicopters do. But when this plane flies, it is much faster than a helicopter.

This plane can land on the ship's small landing field.

A hover boat speeds along, never touching the water.

WATERCRAFT

One of the new ways to travel over water is in a boat that hovers. This boat moves *over* water, not on it or in it. It rides on a cushion of air that keeps the boat above the water.

This is no ordinary boat. It has a flat bottom and a kind of skirt made of rubber. A giant fan pushes air from the top of the craft down inside the rubber skirt. This makes the boat hover over the waves.

An interesting thing about this boat is that it can come out of the water and move over land. It can hover over land just as easily as it hovers over water.

This is a hydrofoil speeding over the water.

Another sort of watercraft is the hydrofoil, which seems to be partly boat and partly plane. Hydrofoils are not new, but new, fast kinds of hydrofoils are now being made. Today many people ride hydrofoils across ponds and lakes.

When a hydrofoil gets going, it lifts itself up. As the craft speeds up, only part of it stays in the water. When you ride in a hydrofoil, all you can see is flying spray as the craft speeds swiftly over the water.

What other new ways of moving around might we have in the future? Perhaps one day we'll have sidewalks that move. If you want to go elsewhere, you will step onto the sidewalk, and it will carry you along.

Or imagine this: it is one hundred years in the future; you wake up one morning and get ready for school. But you do not go downstairs to wait for the bus — there are no buses anymore. Instead you put on a rocket pack. You tell your computer where you want to go. The rocket purrs gently, and you step out of the window and fly to school!

TOMORROW:
Voyages to the Islands of Light

by RICHARD M. CRUM

YESTERDAY

For thousands of years, we have explored the Earth by land, sea, and air. A few years ago, a great new adventure began, when people decided to set forth into the black ocean called *space*. This journey into space has proved to be the most daring of all.

Space is cold, dark, and mostly empty. It is as dark as the darkest cave. The only light comes from the stars, which glow like giant candles in bright colors of red, blue, yellow, and white. There are billions of stars. The one closest to Earth is the sun.

Nine solid bodies move around the sun. These bodies are called *planets*. The sun and the planets make up a space family called the Solar System.

Billions of bodies shine brightly in the night sky. This glow makes the planets and stars look like islands of light. People have long dreamed of traveling to those bright lights to learn more about them. But before the journeys could begin, people had to solve a problem.

Escaping Earth's Gravity

The problem was Earth's gravity. Gravity is like a big magnet that keeps things from floating off the Earth. When people on Earth jump up in the air, they fall back down to the ground. It's gravity that pulls them down.

Earth's gravity is very strong. How can it be over-

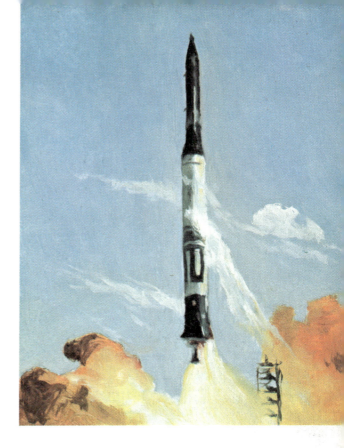

come? A man who lived many years ago had an idea: "Build a spaceship. Put it in a huge gun, and shoot it to the moon." This may seem silly to us now. But the man was right in one way. If you give the ship a large enough push, it will escape Earth's gravity.

People solved the problem of escaping Earth's gravity by building rockets. A rocket sometimes looks like a cone-shaped ship. It moves so swiftly and with so much power that it can pull away from the Earth's atmosphere.

Beep, beep, beep. This sound announced the start of travel into space in 1957. The thing making the "beep" was a metal ball circling the Earth. A rocket had escaped Earth's gravity and had put a radio in space! Scientists called the ball a satellite. A satellite is something that circles around a larger thing. The moon circles around the Earth. It is a satellite, too.

With the satellite, scientists proved that machines could be sent up from Earth into space. But sometimes machines are unreliable. Parts break, or power runs out, and then machines become useless. The answer was to send *people* into space, too.

Could people live in cold, empty space? Yes, if they had special suits and rode in special rocket ships. The suits and ships held in good air and kept out the heat, cold, and other space dangers.

In 1969, two Americans rode a giant rocket into space. They crossed the dark emptiness and became the first people to land on the moon. It was a great day! The journey showed that people could land on a new world. The voyages to the islands of light were well under way.

TODAY

Work in space has changed our lives on Earth. Many things that make our lives better have come from this work to put people in space. One item is a kind of hospital bed sheet that cannot catch fire. House paint that lasts a long time and small pocket radios are two more things. Pots and pans that do not crack with heat or cold came from space work. And the little box that rings when there is smoke in the house was first made for a satellite.

Today, satellites in space are helping us see the Earth in many new ways. They help find water in dry lands. They even look for metals buried deep in the Earth! The weather pictures on your television screen come from space.

Today, communicating is easier, too. Overhead, space satellites speed telephone calls across oceans and around the world. They also send television pictures from one country to another. People can sit at home and watch a show even though it's taking place in a distant land.

TOMORROW

Someday, people will probably live and work in space. They might live in a city in space called a *space station*. Here, new and remarkable discoveries might help us all to live better.

Space station hospitals will probably be very different from those on Earth. A badly burned person will get well much faster and with less pain. He or she will not have to wear dressings that hurt, and will be able to float untouched in a no-gravity hospital room.

People may also begin to explore the moon. Moon rocks hold many metals which could be used to make clean air, water, rocket parts, and tools.

Other riches may be hidden in space. Thousands of tiny bodies called asteroids float in space. Scientists believe that these asteroids may have many metals we need on Earth. Iron might be found in some. One scientist has said that a big asteroid might hold twenty million *million* tons of iron — far more than people have used up to now.

A rocket might push a big asteroid from far away and put it close to Earth. Then space miners could dig out the metals for people on Earth to use.

Perhaps huge telescopes will be set up in space. These telescopes will be pointed at the stars and will show scientists things that are impossible to see from Earth. They may help us learn about other mysteries beyond the Solar System.

The day of discovering all the treasures in space is still far in the future. One reason for this is that today's rockets have one great shortcoming. They are fast enough to escape Earth's gravity, but they are much too slow for journeys through the Solar System. It's a long way to the planets. A trip to a distant planet in our Solar System could take many years. A journey to the stars could be a tedious voyage lasting many lifetimes.

Not long ago, traveling to the islands of light was only a dream. Today, we have touched the moon. People's hopes have been strengthened. They are working hard to reach new islands of light.

Skills Lesson: Sequence, Time Order

What's the Order?

It was the first day of baseball. Maria and Anna were getting ready to play.

"Let's go over the steps before we go out to the field," said Maria.

"That's easy," said Anna. "In baseball, someone bats a ball and someone pitches a ball and runners run the bases."

Maria looked surprised. "Those are the right steps, but they're not in the right order. You have to know the order before you can play the game."

Do you agree with Maria? If you have ever watched or played baseball, you know that Maria is right. You have to know the order of the game.

When you read, you also follow an order. A story only makes sense when the order of what takes place is clear.

Now read to see how Maria explained the order of the game to Anna. Look for the words she used to show the order.

"First, the batter comes up to home plate," said Maria. "Then, the pitcher throws the ball and the batter tries to hit it. If the batter misses, it's a strike. After three strikes, she's

out. But when the batter hits the ball, she runs to first base."

"What happens after you get to first base?" asked Anna.

"Then the next batter comes to home plate. She tries to hit the ball," answered Maria. "If she hits it, the person on first runs to second. Every time someone hits the ball, the players on the bases try to run all the way around the bases to home plate."

Maria used certain words to explain the order of the game to Anna. One of the words is *first*. Can you find the other words?

TRY THIS

Write or tell a friend how to play checkers or another game. Have your friend repeat the directions to you. See if your friend can repeat the steps in the right order.

If you write the steps down, have your friend read them and then tell them to you without looking at the paper.

These words may help you:

before	next
after	when
first	now
then	later
last	finally

ELSA

by JOY ADAMSON

The true story of a lioness who was brought up from cubhood by Joy Adamson and her husband. They taught her to stalk and kill for herself so that she could be set free into the African jungle.

Elsa's story begins one day when my husband George and I were out with our Land Rover. George had gone off into the bush when he was suddenly charged by a wild lioness. He had to kill her. It was while he was looking at the beautiful animal that he understood why she had been so angry. She was guarding her cubs. He searched until he found three tiny lionesses, not more than a few days old. They were hidden down a hole in a rock. He brought the babies back to me and we took them home.

For two days they would not take any milk at all. But once they found out how delicious canned milk was, they could hardly get enough of it.

When the cubs were about ten weeks old, they learned to enjoy the taste of books. We decided to build a door of wire and place it across the door to the house. The cubs did not like this very much, but they soon found plenty to keep them busy outside. They loved to play "King of the Castle" on a potato bag.

Their best toy was a bag filled with old rubber tubes which we tied to a branch. They loved hanging on to it while we pulled and they swung high in the air.

When the cubs were about five months old, we knew that we couldn't keep three fast-growing lions in the house. So we sadly decided that the two bigger ones should be sent to the zoo. We would keep Elsa, who was the smallest and who had the most pleasing manners.

Elsa was very unhappy when her sisters left. She now had to play by herself. We decided to take her with us on a trip. Luckily Elsa loved the outdoor life as much as we did. She often went out on little trips of her own.

Elsa now began to meet other wild animals. She was quite fearless and would chase a whole herd of elephants. She enjoyed stalking giraffes, who did not seem to mind. They just watched while she crawled on her stomach toward them. One day she thought we had spoiled her stalk by standing up and watching her. She got very cross, rushed back, and knocked us both to the ground!

When Elsa was about a year old, we decided to spend some time on the shores of the Indian Ocean. The journey took us three days. As soon as we arrived, we all went down to the beach to show Elsa the sea. To our surprise she loved it. She enjoyed, among many other games, trying to catch a coconut which George swung on a long string.

Later we made another trip, this time to a large lake. It was a long, weary journey of five hundred kilometers, and Elsa traveled in the back of the truck. As soon as we arrived at the lake, she raced into the water. She cooled and cleaned herself from the heat and dust of traveling. She did not worry one bit about the crocodiles, which swam about there in great numbers.

We walked for about seven or eight hours each day. Elsa often swam in the lake to keep cool. She liked walking early in the morning or late in the evening. In the heat of the day, during our afternoon break, she liked to share my camp bed for a short nap.

When we returned home Elsa began to spend more and more time going off on her own. She was nearly two years old. Her voice was getting much deeper. Often she stayed away for two or three days. We knew that she several times joined up with other lions. But she was as friendly as ever when she saw us again.

We now began to wonder whether we could send Elsa back to the wild instead of sending her to join her sisters at the zoo. It would be worth trying. We thought we would take her to a place where there was plenty of game. We would spend two or three weeks with her, and, if all went well, leave her.

Elsa traveled in the back of my truck. The morning after we arrived, we took off her collar to show her that she was free. She hopped onto the roof of the Land Rover and we set off to explore the land.

Elsa had no idea how to kill for food. We decided to leave her where there was plenty of game. We hoped that when she grew hungry she would learn to attack.

But she hated being left on her own. When we came back to her, she was terribly hungry. She had not eaten since our last visit.

We knew we could not leave her yet.

Shortly after this Elsa became very ill and her whole training stopped for the time being.

When she grew better we decided to move to another place. Her new home was only some twenty miles from where we had found her. It was a really beautiful place, with a river running through it where many wild animals came to drink.

Every morning we took Elsa for a walk so that she would get used to the country. If we were only going a short way, she liked to ride on the roof of the Land Rover.

We stayed with her for many months while she learned all the things her own mother would have taught her. At first we did most of the hunting. But she always helped us and soon learned to kill on her own.

From then on, we watched for a chance to leave her. One afternoon she disappeared. We did not see her until the next morning. We knew she had made friends with a wild lion and that the time had now come.

We drove to another river ten miles away where we planned to spend a week. Then we would return and see how she had done without us. I knew it was for her good. But I could not help feeling we were deserting her.

At last the week of waiting ended. On our return we fired a shot. Elsa came rushing out of the bush, overjoyed to see us. She was thin but not hungry. She showed no interest in the meat we had brought her.

After this we often paid Elsa short visits. She was always happy to see us but it was quite plain that she could get along without us. I went to England for a long time that summer. After my return she was very pleased to see me.

We had always hoped that Elsa would find a mate and that one day she would walk into our camp followed by a family.

You can imagine our great joy when a few months later she swam across the river followed by three fine cubs.

Glossary

This glossary is a little dictionary. It contains many of the words found in this book. The glossary tells you how to spell the word, how to pronounce it, and what the word means. Sometimes a different form of the word follows the definition. It appears in boldfaced type. The symbols used to show the pronunciation are explained in the key that follows.

PRONUNCIATION KEY*

a	add, map	m	move, seem	u	up, done
ā	ace, rate	n	nice, tin	û(r)	urn, term
â(r)	care, air	ng	ring, song	yōō	use, few
ä	palm, father	o	odd, hot	v	vain, eve
b	bat, rub	ō	open, so	w	win, away
ch	check, catch	ô	order, jaw	y	yet, yearn
d	dog, rod	oi	oil, boy	z	zest, muse
e	end, pet	ou	out, now	zh	vision, pleasure
ē	even, tree	ōō	pool, food	ə	the schwa,
f	fit, half	ŏŏ	took, full		an unstressed
g	go, log	p	pit, stop		vowel representing
h	hope, hate	r	run, poor		the sound spelled
i	it, give	s	see, pass		a in above
ī	ice, write	sh	sure, rush		e in sicken
j	joy, ledge	t	talk, sit		i in possible
k	cook, take	th	thin, both		o in melon
l	look, rule	th	this, bathe		u in circus

In the pronunciations an accent mark (′) is used to show which syllable of a word receives the most stress. The word *bandage* [band′ij], for example, is stressed on the first syllable. Sometimes there is also a lighter accent mark (′) that shows where there is a lighter stress, as in the word *combination* [kom′bə·nā′shən].

The following abbreviations are used throughout the glossary: *n.*, noun; *v.*, verb; *adj.*, adjective; *adv.*, adverb; *interj.*, interjection; *prep.*, preposition; *conj.*, conjunction; *pl.*, plural; *sing.*, singular.

*Reprinted from *The HBJ School Dictionary*, copyright © 1977, 1972, 1968 by Harcourt Brace Jovanovich, Inc.

adventure   collars

A

adventure [ad·ven′chər] *n.* An exciting or dangerous happening: the *adventure* of climbing mountains.
amazing [ə·māz′ing] *adj.* Very surprising; astonishing.
ancient [ān′shənt] *adj.* Very old.
appeared [ə·pird′] *v.* **1** Came into sight: Two girls *appeared* on the balcony. **2** Seemed: Their reports *appeared* to be true.
aware [ə·wâr′] *adj.* Knowing fully.

B

bagpiper [bag′pī′pər] *n.* A person who plays the bagpipe.
bamboo [bam·bōō′] *n.* A tall, woody grass with a hollow stem.

Bamboo plant

behave [bi·hāv′] *v.* **1** Act correctly: He was told to *behave* and he did. **2** Act: The people *behave* like children.
boar [bôr] *n.* A wild pig.
boardwalk [bôrd′wôk′] *n.* A walk made of boards, often built beside a beach.

C

carved [kärvd] *v.* Cut out of stone, wood, etc.
case [kās] *n.* **1** An action in a court of law. **2** A particular happening: a *case* of robbery.
cells [selz] *n.* Small rooms in a jail.

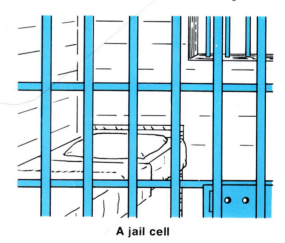

A jail cell

collars [kol′ərz] *n., pl.* Leather straps that are put around animals' necks: dog *collars*.

---

add, āce, câre, pälm;   end, ēqual;   it, īce;   odd, ōpen, ôrder;   tŏŏk, pōōl;   up, bûrn;
ə = a in *above*, e in *sicken*, i in *possible*, o in *melon*, u in *circus*;   yōō = u in *fuse*;   oil;   pout;
ch*eck*;   *r*ing;   *th*in;   *th*is;   zh in *vision*.

commands

commands [kə·mandz'] *n., pl.* Orders.
communicating [kə·myōō'nə·kāt·ing] *v.* 1 Sending messages. 2 Giving and receiving ideas and information.
computers [kəm·pyōō'tərz] *n., pl.* Machines that can do arithmetic very quickly. Computers are often used to control other machines.
cone [kōn] *n.* 1 An object with a round base and a pointed top: The clown is wearing a *cone*-shaped cap. 2 The fruit of the pine tree.

Pine cone

court [kôrt] *n.* A place where law trials are held. *adj. use: court* papers.
crush [krush] *v.* Squeeze a thing until it breaks.
curd [kûrd] *n. (often pl.)* The thick part of sour milk.
cushion [kŏŏsh'ən] *n.* 1 A soft springy material. 2 A bag filled with soft, springy material.

force

D

degrees [di·grēz'] *n., pl.* Units for measuring temperature.
descend [di·send'] *v.* Go down; move to a lower place.
dye [dī] *n.* A liquid used to change the color of things such as clothing.

E

egret [ē'grit] *n.* A white bird that has long, beautiful, white plumes.
empty [emp'tē] *adj.* 1 Not filled: an *empty* seat. 2 Holding nothing: an *empty* jar; *empty* hands.
errand [er'ənd] *n.* A short trip, usually to buy something.
event [i·vent'] *n.* A happening.
excited [ik·sīt'·əd] *v.* Caused strong feelings in: The fireworks *excited* them.

F

faint [fānt] 1 *adj.* Weak or dim: a *faint* light. 2 *v.* Suddenly lose consciousness: The boy may *faint* when he hears the news.
familiar [fə·mil'yər] *adj.* Well known: a *familiar* folktale.
fault [fôlt] *n.* 1 Blame. 2 A crack in the earth where earthquakes can happen.
force [fôrs] 1 *n.* Power or energy; strength: the *force* of the waves. 2 *v.* Move against opposition: to *force* the enemy back into the hills. 3 *v.*

278

forth

Use power to make someone do something: She will *force* them to tell the truth.
forth [fôrth] *adv.* Forward. — **back and forth** first one way, then the opposite way.
future [fyōō′chər] *n.* The time to come; time that will be.

G
---

gasped [gaspt] *v.* Panted; suddenly caught one's breath.
gear [gir] *n.* **1** Equipment: camping *gear*. **2** A wheel used in machines.

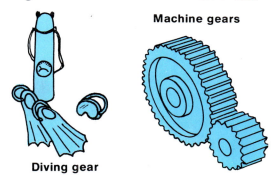

Machine gears

Diving gear

gee [jē] *interj.* A command given to a horse, dog team, etc., meaning "turn to the right."
ghastly [gast′lē] *adj.* **1** *informal* Very bad or unpleasant. **2** Horrible; like a ghost.
glare [glâr] **1** *n.* A bright, blinding light. **2** *n.* An angry look. **3** *v.* Stare angrily.

harness

glossary [glos′ə·rē] *n.* A list of difficult words of a book together with their meanings.
guard [gärd] **1** *v.* Watch over and protect: *guard* a herd. **2** *n.* Someone or something that protects: a palace *guard*; a chain *guard* on a bicycle.
guests [gests] *n., pl.* **1** Visitors. **2** People who come to a meal or party.
guilty [gil′tē] *adj.* Deserving blame for doing wrong.

H
---

habit [hab′it] *n.* Something done so often it becomes automatic.
habitat [hab′ə·tat] *n.* **1** An undersea building in which people live. **2** The place where a plant or animal lives.
harness [här′nis] *n.* Leather straps used to hitch an animal to a cart or plow.

Horse in harness

---

add, āce, câre, pälm; end, ēqual; it, īce; odd, ōpen, ôrder; tŏŏk, pōōl; up, bûrn;
ə = a in *above*, e in *sicken*, i in *possible*, o in *melon*, u in *circus*; yōō = u in *fuse*; oil; pout;
check; ring; thin; this; zh in *vision*.

279

haw

haw [hô] *interj.* A word used by a driver to make a horse, dog team, etc., turn left.
headdress [hed′dres′] *n.* An ornament for the head.
hovers [huv′ərz *or* hov′ərz] *v.* Stays in one place in the air.
hues [hyōōz] *n., pl.* Colors.

I
---

idle [īd′(ə)l] *adj.* Lazy; not willing to work.
item [ī′təm] *n.* One thing in a group of things: an *item* in a list.

J
---

jammed [jamd] *v.* Crowded closely together.
Japan [jə·pan′] *n.* A country made up of several islands east of the Asian mainland.
journey [jûr′nē] **1** *v.* Take a trip. **2** *n.* A trip from one place to another.

L
---

languages [lang′gwij·əz] *n., pl.* The words that groups of people use in speaking and writing.
likeness [līk′nis] *n.* A painting, statue, etc., of a person or thing.
lungs [lungz] *n., pl.* The two organs people use for breathing. The lungs bring oxygen to the blood and remove carbon dioxide from it.

narrator

M
---

manners [man′ərz] *n., pl.* **1** Polite actions: She has nice *manners*. **2** Ways of behaving: Their *manners* were very rude.
measure [mezh′ər] **1** *v.* Find out the size of. **2** *n.* A ruler or scale for finding size: tape *measure*.
mesa [mā′sə] *n.* A hill with a flat top and steep sides, common in the southwestern United States.
mist [mist] *n.* Haze; a cloud of fine drops of water.
motor [mō′tər] *n.* A machine that changes electricity into motion, as in a kitchen blender.

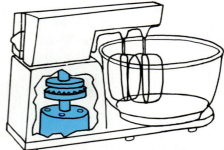

Motor of a kitchen blender

muttered [mut′ərd] *v.* **1** Talked softly through half-closed lips: She *muttered* the answer to the question. **2** Complained; grumbled: They *muttered* against the new rules.

N
---

narrator [na·rāt′ər *or* nar′ā·tər] *n.* A person who talks along with a radio program, film, etc.

nerve

nerve [nûrv] *n.* **1** Courage: to lose one's *nerve*. **2** A part of the body that works like a telephone wire, carrying messages to the brain and muscles.
nods [nodz] *v.* Tips the head down and up.
Nupe [no͞o′pā] A character in an African tale.

O

obey [ō·bā′] *v.* **1** Do as someone wishes: to *obey* one's parents. **2** Follow a command.
ordinary [ôr′də·ner′ē] *adj.* **1** Not unusual in any way: an *ordinary* book. **2** Normal; regular: The *ordinary* price is very high.
overboard [ō′vər·bôrd′] *adv.* Over the side of a ship into the water.

P

panting [pant′ing] *v.* Breathing quickly.
pantomime [pan′tə·mīm] *v.* Act out in body movements without speaking.
pavement [pāv′mənt] *n.* A road with a hard surface.
peace [pēs] *n.* Quiet, calm, or harmony.
peck [pek] *v.* Hit with the beak, as a bird does.

puffing

perch [pûrch] *n.* Branch or roost where something sits.
pit¹ [pit] *n.* A hole dug in the ground.
pit² [pit] *n.* The seed or stone inside a fruit: peach *pit*.
pleaded [plēd′əd] *v.* Begged.
pole¹ [pōl] *n.* A long, thin rod made of wood or metal.
pole² [pōl] *n.* Either end of the earth's axis; the North Pole or the South Pole.

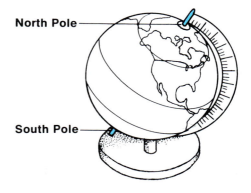

prongs [prôngz] *n., pl.* Pointed parts that stick out.
propeller [prə·pel′ər] *n.* A shaft with blades. The blades turn and drive an airplane, boat, etc., through air or water.
proved [pro͞ovd] *v.* Showed to be true.
pueblos [pweb′lōz] *n., pl.* The stone buildings of the Indians of the southwestern United States.
puffing [puf′ing] *v.* Swelling up: The breezes are *puffing* out the boat's sails.

---

add, āce, câre, pälm;   end, ēqual;   it, īce;   odd, ōpen, ôrder;   to͝ok, po͞ol;   up, bûrn;
ə = a in *above*, e in *sicken*, i in *possible*, o in *melon*, u in *circus*;   yo͞o = u in *fuse*;   oil;   pout;
check;   ring;   thin;   this;   zh in *vision*.

281

pumped

pumped [pumpt] *v.* Lifted a liquid by forcing it up through a pipe.

R

rack [rak] *n.* A frame or stand that holds things: a hat *rack*.

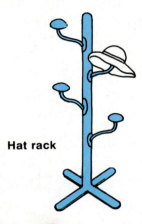

Hat rack

raised [rāzd] *v.* 1 Grew; brought up: They *raised* cattle. 2 Lifted: She *raised* her hand.
rattler [rat′lər] *n.* A rattlesnake.
recipe [res′ə·pē] *n.* Directions for making something to eat.
recovered [ri·kuv′ərd] *v.* 1 Got back; regained: He *recovered* his balance. 2 Got well: She had the flu but she *recovered* quickly.
rejoiced [ri·joisd′] *v.* Was glad.
relations [ri·lā′shənz] *n., pl.* Relatives; persons related by marriage or blood.
repairs [ri·pârz′] *n., pl.* Actions that fix broken things.
reward [ri·wôrd′] *n.* A gift given in thanks for a deed.

screen

roadbed [rōd′bed′] *n.* The base on which a road is built.
rose[1] [rōz] *v.* Went up.
rose[2] [rōz] *n.* A flower with many petals.
rumbles [rum′bəlz] *v.* Makes a low rolling sound like thunder.
runway [run′wā′] *n.* A roadway used by airplanes for take-off and landing.

S

Scotland [skot′lənd] *n.* A part of Great Britain, north of England.

screech [skrēch] *n.* A shrill, harsh cry; shriek.
screen [skrēn] *n.* 1 A smooth surface on which movies or TV programs are shown. 2 A frame of woven wires used to cover windows. 3 Anything that covers or hides things from sight: smoke *screen*.

serious [sir′ē·əs] *adj.* **1** Not joking; sincere: Is she *serious* about the trip? **2** Grave; thoughtful: You look *serious* today.
shafts [shafts] *n., pl.* **1** Pits; deep holes sunk into the earth. **2** Long, narrow rods or bars: arrow *shafts*.
shallow [shal′ō] *adj.* Not deep.
shortcoming [shôrt′kum′ing] *n.* A weakness or failure.
sneers [snirz] *v.* Lifts the upper lip to show contempt.
solid [sol′id] *adj.* **1** Having length, width, and thickness: a *solid* figure. **2** Not liquid or gas: Lava is *solid* after it cools.
sought [sôt] *v.* **1** Tried; attempted: He *sought* to tell his story. **2** Went in search of: They *sought* the buried treasure.
steadily [sted′ə·lē] *adv.* Regularly; without changing or stopping.
strengthened [streng(k)′thənd] *v.* Made stronger.
stretch [strech] **1** *v.* Pull beyond the usual size: Can you *stretch* this rubber band? **2** *v.* Fill an area: The sand dunes *stretch* for miles on all sides. **3** *n.* An area of space: a *stretch* of forest.
surface [sûr′fis] **1** *n.* The outside of a solid: the *surface* of the earth. **2** *n.* The top layer of a liquid: the *surface* of the ocean. **3** *v.* Come to the top, especially of water: Dolphins *surface* in order to breathe.

swivel [swiv′əl] *v.* Turn.
swivel chair [swiv′əl châr] *n.* A chair whose seat turns independently of the base.

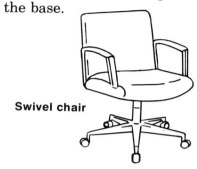
Swivel chair

T

tangled [tang′gəld] *v.* Twisted together in a confusing way.
tedious [tē′dē·əs] *adj.* Long and dull; tiresome.
terror [ter′ər] *n.* Great fear; dread.
thermometer [thər·mom′ə·tər] *n.* A device that measures temperatures.

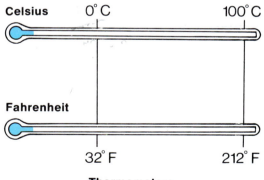
Thermometers

---

add, āce, câre, pälm;   end, ēqual;   it, īce;   odd, ōpen, ôrder;   to͝ok, po͞ol;   up, bûrn;
ə = a in *above*, e in *sicken*, i in *possible*, o in *melon*, u in *circus*;   yo͞o = u in *fuse*;   oil;   pout;
check;   ring;   thin;   this;   zh in *vision*.

283

thump

thump [thump] *n.* **1** A dull, heavy sound. **2** A blow made with something blunt or heavy.

toughened [tuf′ənd] *v.* Made rugged.

tube [t(y)o͞ob] *n.* **1** A tunnel for trains, cars, etc. **2** A long hollow pipe. **3** A pipe of soft metal for holding toothpaste, paint, and so forth. **4** An electronic part that lights up: television *tube.*

U
---

underwent [un′dər·went′] *v.* Lived through; endured.

unreliable [un·ri·lī′ə·bəl] *adj.* Not able to be trusted; undependable.

urged [urjd] *v.* **1** Tried to make someone do something: He *urged* them to try this plan. **2** Drove forcefully: She *urged* the horses on.

V
---

vain [vān] *adj.* **1** Filled with false pride: the *vain* king. **2** Useless; unsuccessful: a *vain* attempt.

voyage [voi′ij] *n.* A journey by water.

W
---

wandered [won′dərd] *v.* **1** Roamed; moved this way and that: They *wandered* through the museum. **2** Strayed: They *wandered* off course.

Washington, D.C. [wäsh′ing·tən *or* wôsh′ing·tən] *n.* The capital of the

xylophone

United States, located in the District of Columbia.

whether [(h)weth′ər] *conj.* If it is true that: We aren't sure *whether* they went to the movies.

whispered [(h)wis′pərd] *v.* Spoke in a soft, low voice.

whoa [(h)wō] *interj.* A word used by a driver to make a horse, dog team, etc., come to a stop.

worn [wôrn] **1** *adj.* Damaged by much use or wear. **2** *adj.* Tired; weary. **3** *v.* Carried on the body as clothes or decoration: A hat is *worn* on the head.

worth [wûrth] **1** *prep.* Deserving: a place *worth* a visit. **2** *n.* The value of anything in money.

X
---

xylophone [zī′lə·fōn] *n.* A musical instrument with wooden bars that are hit with hammers.

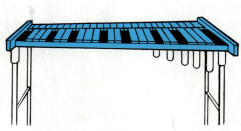

Xylophone

284

New Words

PAGES 10–21

camel
hump
among
desert
humph
neighed
yoke
Djinn
idle°
since
chin
obey°
puffing°
behave°
yet
crocodiles
Oki
ancient°
hare
mainland
life
often
manners°
compared
rose°
choke
repeated
vain°
bridge
leaped
snapped

stump
bushy

PAGES 22–35

whether°
plenty
hours
coin
sniffing
paid
serious°
fists
banged
owe
court°
judge
guilty°
silver
case°
courtroom
flooded
laughter
understood

PAGES 36–43

Yuji
bamboo°
Japan°
voice
distant
faint°
warm
stretch°
whoosh
swoosh
pine

thump°
measure°

PAGES 44–49

cattle
egret°
Nupe°
pastures
glare°
Kanda
despair
insects
earn
reward°
perch°
throats
urged°
beak
peck°
clear
gushed
drank
less
peace°
guard°

PAGES 50–61

xylophone°
gong
boar°
music
pantomime°
charges
growling
sneers°
nods°
double

force°
clever
pit°
fanning
stage
nose
terror°

PAGES 66–71

Elsa
Baffia
habit°
admit
chance
drawings
stairs
frowned
mistake
oxen
questions
rack°
prongs°
middle
built
women

PAGES 72–79

mystery
oak
buried
special
succeeded
east
thick
boards
fifty
Lynds

Words marked ° appear in glossary.

hired
crew
uncovered
pumped°
sideways
drilling
Blair
written
anyway
dye°
Gilbert Hedden
shafts°

PAGES 80–86

unbelievable
cousin
enables
travelers
fleas
impolite
quite
height
terns
Arctic
spends
months
pole°
south
spring
Alaskan
distance
avoid
cheetah
antelope
jungle
attack
thermometer°

cricket
chirping
degrees°

PAGES 87–92

Harry Houdini
magician
amazing°
ordinary°
enjoyment
amazement
magical
escape
jail
useless
proved°
cells°
Washington, D.C.°
several
minutes
beforehand
searched
glue
crate
appeared°
sharp

PAGES 98–105

Fallah's
tent
guests°
already
ghastly°
thirsty
harness°

swung
muttered°
rather
breath

PAGES 108–114

sought°
share
chalks
familiar°
Eskimo
simple
stall
straw
overflowing
delicious
ripe
inviting
Bom Bosh
Bushongo
country
likeness°
carved°
headdress°
circle
countryside
Yugoslavia
halfway

PAGES 115–129

Robin
Nubbin
chained
Flip
Flop
gee°
haw°

commands°
toughened°
excited°
collars°
unchained
ahead
panting°
moose
whew
tangled°
whoa°
announcer's
hugged

PAGES 130–143

Wee Gillis
Scotland°
Alastair
 Roderic
 Craigellachie
 Dalhousie
 Gowan
 Donny-bristle
 MacMac
relations°
Lowlanders
valleys
raised°
Highlanders
both
mist°
lungs°
sigh
Angus
choose
pleaded°

286

begged
cheeks
bagpiper°
aye
screech°
welcome

PAGES 144–158

Taro
tofu
evening
bean
curd°
direction
beyond
dim
alone
grandson
yen
errand°
candy
chocolate
extra
whispered°
fault°
shy
ached

PAGES 162–171

unknown
India
ninety
choice
adventure°

beads
August
Niña
Pinta
Santa María
journey°
voyage°
September
surrounded
complained
bunches
ahoy
overboard°
silk
allow
October
moonrise
candle
o'clock
rejoiced°
San Salvador

PAGES 172–181

Amelia Earhart
Atlantic
ninth
event°
airplane
papa
broad
thin
winglike
motor°
hooked
speeding

silence
swooped
cost
lessons
suit
contact
propeller°
runway°
gasped°
hues°
Netta Snook
controls
possibly
dollhouses
diving
huge
bump

PAGES 184–189

explorer
worn°
mesa°
Estevan
Estevanico
Cibola
Southwest
whose
Spanish
meant
kid
Steve
Florida
Spaniards
underwent°
except
wandered°
languages°

fabulous
rattler°
meanwhile
perhaps
camp
pueblos°
Zuñi

PAGES 194–201

pillow
encyclopedia
detective
neighborhood
beech
Danny
boardwalk°
Meany
railing
posts
clothesline
trap
smart
fellow
rode
cards
brain
recovered°
mind
nerve°
yard
heel

PAGES 202–204

effects
radio
blood
chilling

287

moans
rumbles°
remarkably
cookie
footsteps
creaky
brick
bend
pouring
FM
empty°
hiss
steadily°
soda
squeaking
swivel°
telephone

PAGES 205–211

haunted
eerie
narrator°
gusts
David
ghost
scaredy
worth°
awfully
clap
closet
slams
frightened
imagine

PAGES 212–221

Nate
vacation
Sludge
pancake
Claude
losing
list
butter
sugar
tuna
map
drew
solve
whichever
pavement°
Rosamond's
recipe°
curious
taste
powder
eleven
apart
forcefully
twelve

PAGES 226–237

inventions
surface°
unfamiliar
crush°
craft
descend°
submarines

computers°
shallow°
gear°
habitat°
future°
tame
misbehave
oil
encircle
tag
picnic
unimaginable

PAGES 238–249

jammed°
probably
aware°
electric
repairs°
buttons
roadbed°
highway
cushion°
tube°
jets
silently
hovers°
skirt
hydrofoil
elsewhere
instead

PAGES 250–256

forth°
solid°

planets
gravity
magnet
cone°
beep
satellite
unreliable°
item°
weather
television
screen°
communicating°
pain
asteroids
iron
tons
shortcoming°
tedious°
strengthened°

PAGES 261–275

lioness
cubhood
Adamson
George
Rover
cubs
spoiled
arrived
coconut
nap
drove
meat
mate

288